lone

POCKET
SEATTLE

Sarah Etinas

Contents

Above: Kayaking, Lake Union (p95)
Below: Cherry blossoms, Quad at UW (p116)

FROM TOP LEFT: OKSANA PERKINS/SHUTTERSTOCK, GEORGECOLEPHOTO/SHUTTERSTOCK

The Journey Begins Here

Seattle can sometimes feel like it's always changing. Big-name businesses seem to emerge one after the other, transforming the skyscraper-filled downtown as they expand. Microbreweries, coffee roasters and experimental restaurants are put through the high-rent gauntlet, with some surviving for decades and others disappearing not long after opening. Yet even amid all this flux, Seattle's core – one of kindness, both to others and the planet – is constant. Cultural communities share the flavors of their ancestry in family-owned restaurants, rainbow flags fly proudly over LGBTIQ+-owned businesses, and nature-loving locals leave greenspaces better than they find them. It's a city more than worth exploring.

Sarah Etinas

sarahetinas.com

Sarah is a freelance travel writer and editor. Find her exploring the world one sunny beach and innovative restaurant at a time.

Seattle skyline and Mount Rainier (p154)

AGNIESZKA GAUL/SHUTTERSTOCK

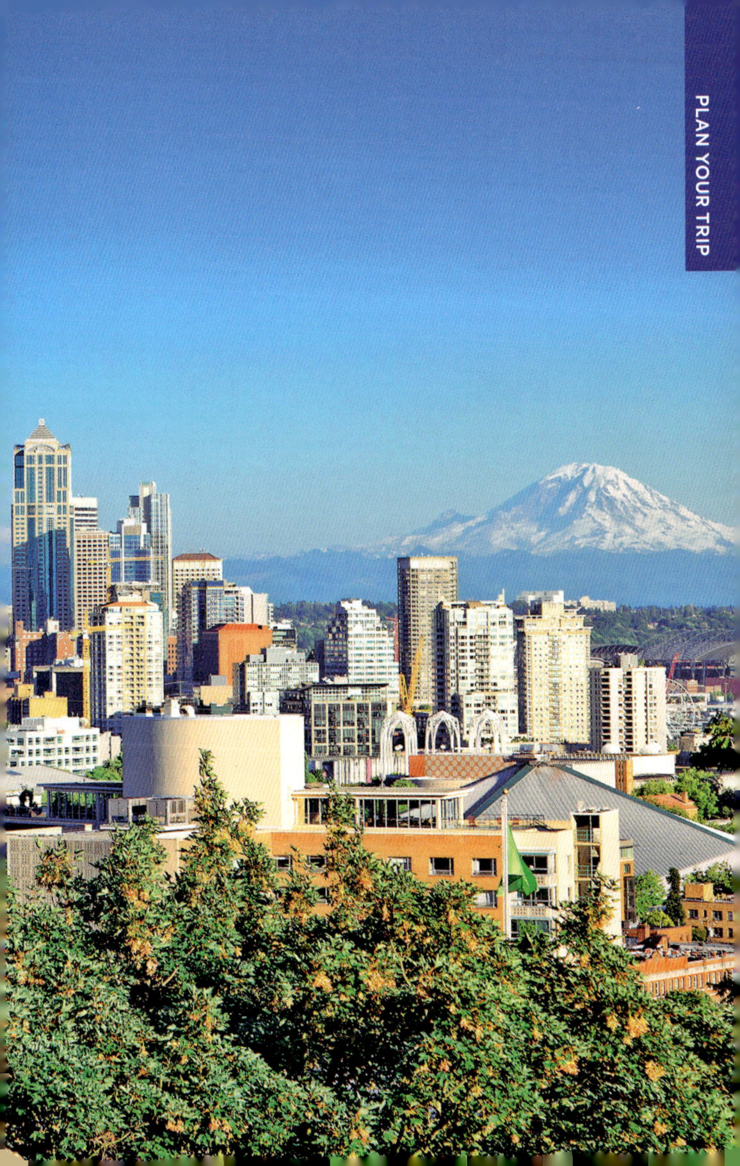

THE BEST

On the Water

From Puget Sound to Lake Union to Lake Washington, Seattle is surrounded by water. Why not take advantage of that fact – and the Seattle summer sunshine – with water activities galore?

Kayak your way around **Washington Park Arboretum** for beautiful blooms and unbeatable water views. (p116)

Take in the Seattle skyline from the water by sailing with **Argosy Cruises** on Puget Sound. (p45; pictured)

Heat your worries away as you sail on Lake Union via a wood-fired sauna boat, courtesy of **Wild Haus Floating Saunas**. (p104)

Enjoy a completely free boat ride on Lake Union each Sunday with the **Center for Wooden Boats**, departing from Lake Union Park. (p94)

Take to the water and to the skies with **Kenmore Air**'s Seattle Scenic Seaplane Tour. (p94; pictured)

Set sail from the Eastside on beautiful Lake Washington with **Bellevue Lake Cruises**. (p148)

Right: Centre for Wooden Boats (p94), Lake Union

FROM LEFT: UTE SONJA MEDLEY/SHUTTERSTOCK, VICTORIA DITKOVSKY/SHUTTERSTOCK, AMEHIME/SHUTTERSTOCK

THE BEST

Urban Nature Gems

Get outdoors and enjoy the best of Seattle's gorgeous natural beauty – from its parks to its botanical gardens and everything in between.

Hike through **Discovery Park**'s 12-mile trail network, enjoying the best of its Puget Sound and Olympic Mountain views. (p94)

Stroll among centuries-old evergreens at West Seattle's **Schmitz Preserve Park**. (p139)

Admire the views of Lake Washington, Mount Rainier and beyond from **Seward Park** in South Seattle. (p128; pictured)

Stop and smell the flowers – irises, dahlias, fuschia and hydrangeas – at the stunning (and free) **Bellevue Botanical Garden**. (p148; pictured)

Get away to **Mount Rainier National Park** for a day trip, where greenery-filled hikes and unbeatable mountain views await. (p154)

Right: Mount Rainier National Park (p154)

THE BEST

Local Shopping

Like any big US city, Seattle has a whole host of big-name stores. More precious and of more interest are the locally owned, one-of-a-kind shops you'll find hidden down alleys and crammed between coffee shops.

Stroll through Seattle's iconic shopping area, **Pike Place Market**, where hundreds of vendors sell everything from clam chowder to handmade leather shoes. (p46; pictured)

Support local artists at **Seattle Waterfront Marketplace**, a collective selling everything from watercolor paintings to floral soaps. (p53)

Admire Native American artistry firsthand at **Eighth Generation**, a new addition to Seattle's downtown owned by the Snoqualmie Tribe. (p53)

Experience the tradition of a weekend farmers market visit with a trip to **Ballard Farmers Market**, home to 100+ vendors. (p116; pictured)

Get yourself some 'unfortunate' cookies (misshapen fortune cookies) from the fourth-generation family-owned **Tsue Chong Retail Store**. (p69)

Purchase a record from a new-to-you artist at West Seattle's **Easy Street Records & Cafe**, arguably the city's most multifarious record store. (p137)

THE BEST

Reader Realm

Seattle is one of just two UNESCO Cities of Literature in the US, and with the numerous libraries, bookstores and publishing houses spread across the city, there's really no question of why this literature-loving city was given this esteemed title.

Pop into arguably the most well-known bookstore in the city: **Elliott Bay Book Company**. Located in Capitol Hill, it has over 150,000 titles and an incredibly inclusive selection. (p101)

Find your next read – new or used – at **Third Place Books**. Then, settle in to read it at the on-site cafe or pub. (p121)

Pay a visit to **Day Moon Press**, a cozy family-owned letterpress print shop with loads of old-school printmaking gear and a small retail section. (p131)

Experience the best of books and bites at Fremont's **Book Larder**, a North Seattle gem with shelves stocked to the brim with cookbooks. (p121)

Get equipped for your next trip at **Metsker Maps**. This nearly century-old shop is filled with maps, globes and travel guidebooks galore. (p53)

Elliott Bay Book Company (p101)

THE BEST

Gleaming Glass Art

Some say that Seattle has a 'heart of glass' with all of its glass attractions and studios. Take your time admiring the work of the pros or try your hand at a glass-blown creation.

Soak in the beauty of its flowery, 100ft-long hanging sculpture at **Chihuly Garden & Glass**, the icon of the Seattle glass scene. (p78; pictured)

Explore beyond the works of Dale Chihuly at neighboring Tacoma's **Museum of Glass**, where several prominent glass artists display their creations. (p152)

Try glass blowing for yourself with the beginner-friendly classes at Ballard's **Blowing Sands Glass**. Before you know it, you'll have made your very own beautiful ornament, drinking glass or vase! (p116)

Snag a few handmade, colorful glass cups from **glassybaby** to add a touch of Seattle artistry to your home. (p147)

Right: Museum of Glass, Tacoma (p152)

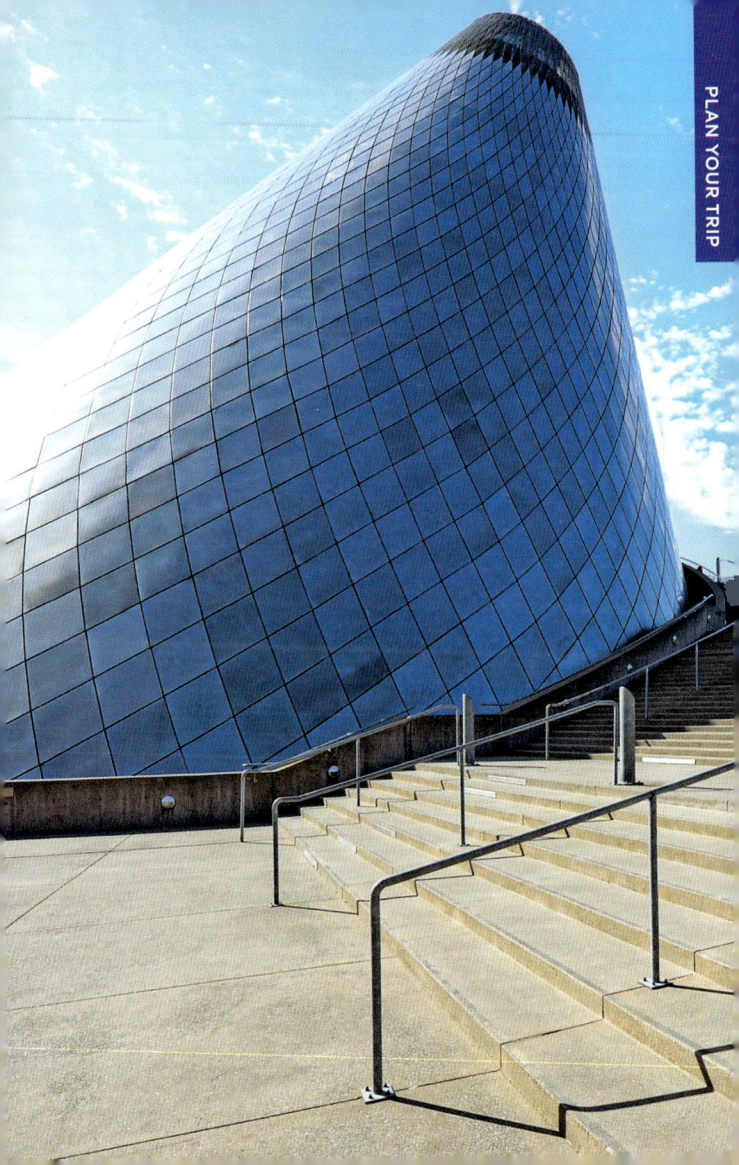

THE BEST

Brewed, Vinified & Distilled

Whether you're into beer, wine, cider or hard liquor, Seattle's got a small local artisan crafting and pouring something special for you. Find your new favorite drink anywhere from an industrial distillery to a Versailles-inspired winery.

Take your taste buds to Italy at SoDo's **Letterpress Distilling**, where liqueurs like amaro and limoncello are the stars of the show. (p68)

Sip on some of the finest whiskey in town – on its own or in cocktail form – at **Westland Distillery**. (p68)

Sample beers with all sorts of fun flavor notes, from gingerbread to Buddha's hand citrus, at **Lucky Envelope Brewing**. (p113)

Enjoy the crispness of PNW apples in drink form at **Schilling Cider House**. Beyond the simple, fresh pome fruit flavors, it also has more adventurous options, such as habanero lime and lavender bergamot. (p121)

Enjoy Washington-made wines and concerts from big-name artists at the French-inspired **Chateau St Michelle**. (p149; pictured)

Starbucks Reserve Roastery (p104)

THE BEST

Coffee Culture

Every rainy day in this city is just another opportunity to warm up with a cup of joe. Seattle practically invented modern North American coffee culture, thanks to a small store in Pike Place Market that went global: Starbucks.

In Downtown Seattle, **FUTUREBEAN by Storyville Coffee** serves impeccable mochas and salted caramel cookies are the perfect way to start the day. (p52)

Get a taste of arguably the best espresso in the city at Capitol Hill's **Espresso Vivace**. (p106)

Sip on an expertly crafted cup of coffee at **Milstead & Co**, a fabulous Fremont coffee bar that selects its beans with the precision of a French sommelier. (p120)

Start your day with **Victrola Coffee Roasters**' 4oz cappuccino that's as small as it is delicious. (p131)

Venture to Little Saigon where the baristas at **Phin** brew fantastic condensed-milk-drizzled Vietnamese coffee drinks. (p67)

Dive deeper into the world of coffee at the **Starbucks Reserve Roastery**, where coffee flights and espresso-martini-making classes are just the beginning. (p104)

THE BEST

Weird & Wonderful

While Portland often garners all the attention with its unconventional nature, Seattle also has its fair share of weirdly wonderful gems. You'll find more than a few quirky shops, art installations and even an out-of-the-box museum or two.

Leave your mark in the form of a chewing gum wad at Seattle's **Gum Wall**, a grossly popular selfie spot. (p46; pictured)

Spot a century-old mummy tucked behind $10 oddities at the back of **Ye Olde Curiosity Shop**. (p45)

Say hello to artist Thomas Dambo's five trolls dotted around the greater Seattle area, starting with **Bruun Idun** in West Seattle's Lincoln Park. (p139)

Play through the decades of pinball history at the International District's **Seattle Pinball Museum**. (p63; pictured)

Right: Bruun Idun by Thomas Dambo (p139)

THE BEST
Dining Experiences

Locally sourced ingredients are often the star of Seattle's eateries, with fresh seafood and meaty mushrooms commonly featured on plates. Beyond these PNW staples, the city welcomes flavors from across the globe, with Asian flavors making a particularly strong impression.

Savor PNW flavors at their finest – with a bit of a Filipino spin – at **Archipelago Seattle**. (p130)

Experience Seattle's take on Japanese teriyaki at the chain that started it all: **Toshi's Teriyaki**. (p119)

Take a ferry to Bainbridge Island for the unbeatable handmade pastas and wood-fired pizzas of **Via Rosa 11**. (p55)

Slurp down some of the freshest oysters in town at **Taylor Shellfish Oyster Bar**. (p105)

Splurge on a seasonally inspired *omakase* (chef's choice) meal at the Michelin-worthy **Ltd Edition Sushi**. (p106)

Half-shell shucked oysters

LARRY ZHOU/SHUTTERSTOCK

Jaw-Dropping Views

On a sunny day, Seattle views can't be beat. There's the city with its modern glass skyscrapers serving as markers of technological innovation, but there's also the sparkling Puget Sound and snow-capped Cascade and Olympic Mountain ranges, showing off their natural beauty.

Rise to the top of Seattle's most popular viewpoint – the **Space Needle**, of course – for epic, open-air views from 520ft up. (p76; pictured)

Spot some of the best views of the Space Needle, Downtown Seattle and Elliott Bay from the picture-perfect **Kerry Park** in Magnolia. (p93)

Take in the views from the tallest viewpoint in the city: the 932ft **Columbia Center**. Even better, you'll actually get the Space Needle in your bird's-eye-view photos. (p50)

Hitch a ride on any of the Puget Sound ferries – the one to **Bainbridge Island**, for example – for incredible views of the city, the waterway and the surrounding mountain ranges. (p54)

Get up close and personal with the gorgeous Mount Rainier from **Ricksecker Point**, a road cut out within the national park with some of the best views of the famed peak. (p157; pictured)

FROM LEFT: GRINDSTONE MEDIA GROUP/SHUTTERSTOCK, PAULA COBLEIGH/SHUTTERSTOCK

19

Sustainability at its Finest

Sustainability is woven into the fabric of Seattle and the mindsets of its residents. Vintage stores and zero-waste shops flourish in nearly every neighborhood, and even its public transportation isn't too shabby – a nearly unheard of feat in the US.

Catch a Seattle Kraken hockey game at **Climate Pledge Arena**, where captured rainwater is used to make its sustainable ice hockey rink. (p85; pictured)

Take a tour of the **Bullitt Center**, a Capitol Hill commercial office building that generates more energy than it uses. (p104)

Stock your shelves with preloved reads from nearly any genre from **Third Place Books** in North Seattle. (p121)

Shop to your heart's content at the **Barn Owl Vintage Goods** in Georgetown, where the well-organized and well-curated racks are filled with everything from trendy tees to cowboy boots. (p127)

Right: Bullitt Center (p104)

THE BEST

Places to Get Your Game On

When it comes to professional sports, Seattle has some of the most passionate fans around. The pros are one part of the excitement, but the crowds – dressed in team gear, shouting chants at the top of their lungs – make the experience even better.

Catch a game at **Lumen Field** – home to the Seattle Seahawks (NFL), the Seattle Reign (NWSL) and the Seattle Sounders (MLS) – and experience the energy of the fans firsthand. (p63; pictured)

Sailgate – aka tailgate on a boat – on Lake Washington before catching a football game at UW's **Husky Stadium**. (p117)

Watch the Seattle Mariners (MLB) play on a real grass field at the retro-style **T-Mobile Park**. (p64; pictured)

Cheer on two incredible teams – the Seattle Kraken (NHL) and the Seattle Storm (WNBA) – at the sustainable **Climate Pledge Arena**. (p85)

Best for Kids

Spend a day at the **Woodland Park Zoo** (p118), where hundreds of animals roam free in their eco-system enclosures rather than being stuck in restrictive cages.

Make a few new marine friends – otters, seahorses and a Giant Pacific octopus, just to name a few – at the new and improved **Seattle Aquarium** (p45).

Watch boats rise and fall with the water levels at the **Ballard Locks** (p114), a captivating feat of engineering for people of all ages.

Introduce your little ones to the joy of old-school pinball at the International District's **Seattle Pinball Museum** (p63).

Take your pilots-in-the-making to the captivating **Museum of Flight** (p128), where landmarks of aerospace travel – including Apollo lunar modules and the first Boeing 747 – reside.

Best for Free

Spend an afternoon at the **Ballard Locks** (p114), where boats rise and fall with the water levels and salmon jump their way up the fish ladders.

Escape into nature at **Discovery Park** (p94), where 12 miles of trails and epic Puget Sound views await.

Cross over Lake Washington to the Eastside, where the lovely **Bellevue Botanical Garden** (p148) thrives with colorful blooms all spring and summer long.

Save your Sunday morning for a free boat ride on Lake Union with the **Center for Wooden Boats** (p94). Pair your sailing with a lovely afternoon at Lake Union Park.

Shop local at the **North Seattle farmers market scene** (p116), where vendors sell everything from fresh organic produce to warm bread loaves to blooming flower bouquets.

Perfect Days

Make the best of a short trip to Seattle by hitting up the most popular attractions, like the Space Needle and Pike Place Market, and eating your way through the best bites in town.

Space Needle (p76)

DAY ONE

Only Have One Day?

MORNING

Start at **Pike Place Market** (p46) and spend the morning getting lost, browsing, tasting, buying and bantering with the producers. Don't miss the **Gum Wall** (p47) or the **salmon tossing** (p46). Grab a bite to eat at **Beecher's** (p48; pictured) and enjoy your cheesy meal at the **Overlook Walk** (p45) or **Victor Steinbrueck Park** (p49), taking in the Puget Sound views.

AFTERNOON

Take the monorail to Seattle Center, where you'll spend the afternoon admiring the views at the top of the **Space Needle** (p76) and the art at **Chihuly Garden and Glass** (p78).

EVENING

Enjoy the best of Belltown's nightlife scene, catching a performance at the **Pacific Northwest Ballet** (p84) or a jazz act at **Dimitriou's Jazz Alley** (p84).

DAY TWO

A Weekend Trip

MORNING

Kick off day two with a kayaking adventure in North Seattle, departing from the **Agua Verde Paddle Club** (p116) and looping your way around the islands and waterways of the **Washington Park Arboretum** (p116; pictured).

AFTERNOON

Devour a lunch of fish and chips at **Pacific Inn Pub** (p119) in Fremont, before continuing west to the **Ballard Locks** (p114). Watch this feat of engineering in action as it rises and lowers the water levels, and catch the quickest glimpse of fish hopping the salmon ladder.

EVENING

Stick around Ballard for an evening of craft brews from places like the innovative **Lucky Envelope Brewing** (p113) and the long-time-favorite **Reuben's Brews** (p113).

DAY THREE

A Short Break

MORNING

Make your way to the Chinatown-International District, snapping a few pictures at the **Historic Chinatown Gate** (p61) and the tucked-away **Union Station** (p61). Eat a delicious modern Filipino lunch at **Hood Famous Cafe + Bar** (p68).

AFTERNOON

Take the First Hill streetcar line up to Capitol Hill for a behind-the-scenes tour and tasting at the **Starbucks Reserve Roastery** (p104; pictured). Stop in at a few artsy shops, like **Elliott Bay Book Company** (p101) and **Wall of Sound** (p101), while you're in the neighborhood.

EVENING

Dine on a fresh seafood dinner at **Taylor Shellfish Oyster Bar** (p105). Then, experience the best of Capitol Hill's nightlife, dancing the night away at LGBTIQ+ friendly **Unicorn** (p103) or laughing until you cry at **Club Comedy Seattle** (p104).

If You Have More Time

Check what's on in the city during your visit. Sporting events are always a good time, no matter if it's the Seattle Kraken taking to the ice of the **Climate Pledge Arena** (p85) or the Seahawks racing down the lengths of **Lumen Field** (p63). Don't miss the weekend farmers markets, like the ones in **Ballard** (p116) and **West Seattle** (p138), where you'll find some of the best locally made wares.

With a few more days, you'll also have more time for tours. Sail across Puget Sound, taking in the views of the Seattle waterfront, with **Argosy Cruises** (p45). Head below the surface with a tour of the city's 19th-century abandoned underground with **Bill Speidel's Underground Tour** (p63). Or learn more about sustainability with a tour of the ultra-ecofriendly **Bullitt Center** (p104).

There's also the option to cross Lake Washington and explore Seattle's Eastside. Spend a day strolling through the blooms at **Bellevue Botanical Garden** (p148), bird-watching at **Juanita Bay Park** (p148) and sampling delicious blends at the French-inspired **Chateau St Michelle Winery** (p149).

Ducks, Juanita Bay Park (p148)

BILL PERRY/SHUTTERSTOCK

A City Day Trip

Rent a car and drive out to **Mount Rainier National Park** (p154). Spend your day in the **Paradise district** (p154), where the beauty changes with the seasons, with blooming wildflowers in the summer, juicy huckleberries in the fall, and snow-covered landscapes in the winter.

Even so, there are certain activities that you can enjoy (almost) any time of year. Gape in awe at the 180ft **Narada Falls** (p156; pictured), cascading between a stone bridge, and take in particularly stunning views of Mount Rainier from **Ricksecker Point** (p156). If you're up for a hike (or snowshoeing adventure, if it's winter), tackle the short-and-sweet 1.2-mile **Nisqually Vista Trail** (p154), keeping your eyes peeled for wildlife along the way.

On a Rainy Day

There are plenty of rainy days in Seattle, and luckily that means that there are also plenty of indoor things to do. Numerous museums are dotted around, including **MoPOP** (p80), the **Seattle Art Museum** (p50), the **Museum of History & Industry** (p95) and the **Museum of Flight** (p128; pictured), which all make for a great day indoors.

Alternatively, embrace the city's artistic side. Take a glass-blowing class at **Blowing Sands Glass** (p116), making a vase or ornament with your very own hands. Pop into the many **art galleries** (p68) of Pioneer Square. Or catch an indie film – bucket of locally beloved chocolate popcorn in hand – at **SIFF Cinema Downtown** (p83).

Get Prepared

BOOK AHEAD

Several months before Snag tickets to the biggest events for the best prices – think Bumbershoot and A-list Chateau St Michelle Winery concerts.

Two weeks before If you're visiting during peak season, reserve tickets for Seattle's most popular attractions, like the Space Needle and Chihuly Garden and Glass.

One week before Secure tickets to sporting events and make reservations at trendy local restaurants.

Manners Matter

While Seattleites sometimes have a reputation for being closed-off (hello, Seattle freeze), it's really introversion, rather than rudeness. They're often as kind and respectful as they come, and that's a mindset visitors will want to adopt as well. Opt for public transportation when possible – and don't be too loud while aboard. Leave natural spaces better than you find them. Most importantly, be kind to everyone who crosses your path, no matter their background.

Rules of the Road

While Seattle roads are often squishy and pothole-filled, the local drivers more than make up for it with their kindness. They'll make room to let you into their line if you signal, and merging is usually a breeze. If you choose to drive your way around the city, be sure to give your share of kindness on the road as well.

Things to Know

Sustainability is an important part of day-to-day Seattle life, so be prepared to do the little things to contribute. Bring a reusable water bottle. Use a reusable bag for all your shopping needs. Properly dispose of your trash in the appropriate bins, whether it be garbage, recycling or compost.

It's Pike Place Market, not Pike's Place. Using the latter will mark you as a tourist or a recent transplant.

Despite the amount of rain Seattle gets, locals rarely use umbrellas. Unless it's a downpour, jacket hoods are a go-to. While using the former in light rain may let locals know that you're a visitor, feel free to do what suits you best. After all, there's a reason why so many accommodations provide complimentary umbrellas for guests.

TIPPING

Seattleites are generally generous tippers, frequently giving 20% or more at sit-down restaurants and sometimes even at counter-service spots and food trucks. However, a small but growing number of businesses in the city are moving away from tipping by including service costs in their pricing and declining additional gratuities.

DAILY BUDGET

Budget: Less than $150

- Dorm bed in a hostel: **$40–65**
- Pike Place Market take-out small bites: **$15**
- Certain days at museums: **free**
- Public transportation average fare: **$6**

Midrange: $150–300

- Online deal at a no-frills hotel: **$130–190**
- Pub, bakery or sandwich-bar meal: **around $15**
- Cheap tickets for sports games: **from $35**
- Short taxi trip: **$15–20**

Top end: More than $300

- Downtown hotel room: **more than $250**
- Meal at a trendy Capitol Hill restaurant: **from $50**
- Tickets to the theater or a concert: **from $40**

Currency
US dollar ($)

Language
English

Time zone
Pacific Standard Time (GMT/UGC minus eight hours)

TIP

If you plan on hitting up many of the major Seattle attractions – the Space Needle, Chihuly Garden and Glass, and the Seattle Aquarium, just to name a few – consider purchasing the CityPass to save a few bucks.

📅 When To Go

While summer is prime time to visit Seattle – that's when you get sunny weather perfect for hitting up all the nature spots – there's something to do in this PNW city in every season.

There's a reason that summer is peak season in Seattle – its sunny skies are ideal for sailing on Puget Sound and hiking through urban parks.

Fall has its fair share of pull too, with crisp temperatures bringing warm-colored leaves to trees and fresh apples to farmers markets. While winter can be cloudy, it's a wonderful time to snowshoe through Mt Rainier National Park or cozy up with a cup of coffee. By the time rainy spring rolls around, everyone's making the most of the rare sunny day, visiting local botanical gardens and strolling through blooming cherry blossoms.

The Big Events

December/January Kick off the new year with a bang at **New Year's at the Needle** (p84). Watch the Space Needle light up the night sky with both drones and pyrotechnics as you count down until midnight.

June One day a year, Capitol Hill goes all out to celebrate the LGBTIQ+ community during **Seattle PrideFest** (p103), an event filled with talented performers and a wonderful sense of community.

July Sample delicious food and drinks from local Seattle restaurants and vendors at the massively popular **Bite of Seattle** (p84).

August/September Experience the best of the arts at **Bumbershoot** (p84), an internationally renowned, multi-disciplinary arts and music festival. Over the years, greats like Kendrick Lamar, Tina Turner and Jerry Seinfield have all taken to the stage.

Seattle Weather

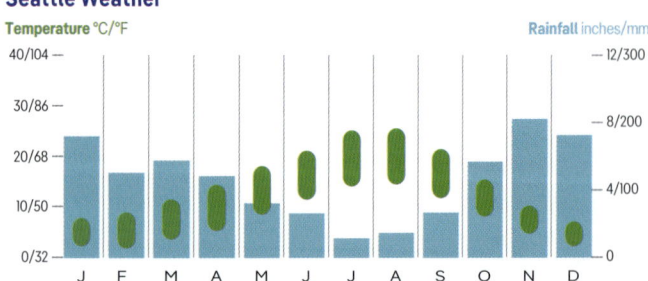

JSIM2018/SHUTTERSTOCK

Whale-watching, Puget Sound (p85)

Changing with the Seasons

March & April Starting in late March, delicate pink and white cherry blossoms bloom all across the city – but most famously at the University of Washington's **Quad** (p116), where dozens of trees are clustered together.

May–September With the sun of summer comes epic concerts at the **Chateau St Michelle Winery** (p149). James Taylor, Stevie Wonder, Kelsea Ballerini and the Goo Goo Dolls are just a few of the talented musicians who have performed here.

May–October While orcas can be seen year-round in Puget Sound, the warmer months of the year welcome other whale species, including humpback and minke, making it prime time for **whale-watching** (p85).

June–September Head to the **Ballard Locks** (p114) and watch the salmon jump their way up the fish ladder, traveling from salt water into fresh water.

ACCOMMODATIONS LOWDOWN

Since summer is the most popular season to visit Seattle, accommodations prices are often highest then. Spring and fall balance prices and weather, while the colder temperatures and cloudy skies of winter bring the most affordable accommodations.

✈ Getting There

Most visitors to Seattle arrive via Seattle-Tacoma International Airport (SEA), more commonly known as Sea-Tac. Some also travel to the city through smaller regional airports, or via train or by boat.

From the Airport to the City Center

By Light Rail

The light rail is by far the most convenient and cost-effective mode of transportation for traveling between Sea-Tac and most Seattle neighborhoods. The Sea-Tac/Airport station is located just outside of Terminal D (save your energy and take intra-airport transportation to get there), connected via a 0.3-mile walkway. The journey to the heart of Seattle takes about 40 minutes (to South Seattle, it's about 20 minutes and to North Seattle, just under an hour). One-way fares cost $3.

By Rideshare or Taxi

If speed is of the essence (and it's nowhere near rush hour),

a rideshare or taxi is a good option. It only takes about 20 minutes to get from Sea-Tac to downtown Seattle via this mode of transportation. But with speed comes priciness, with the average taxi ride costing $40 to $50 and the average rideshare costing $50 to $60.

By Bus

If you're traveling to certain parts of Seattle's Eastside and want to take public transportation, the public bus system may be your best bet, and will likely be used in conjunction with one of the two light rail lines. The journey will likely take at least an hour and cost between $3 and $6.

Other Points of Entry

There are a very limited number of flights into and out of Paine Field (PAE) and King County International Airport (BFI). Beyond air travel, Seattle welcomes thousands of visitors every year traveling via train and boat. The King St Amtrak Station in the International District offers a direct rail link to cities like Portland, Vancouver and even as far as Chicago. Alternatively, the Port of Seattle regularly welcomes cruise ships from all along the West Coast – from California to British Columbia, Canada – with a few vessels coming from as far as Hawaii and Australia. There's also a direct ferry between Seattle and Victoria, British Columbia.

Getting Around

Seattle has many types of public transport – on both land and water. This extensively integrated system of light rails, street cars, monorails, buses, water taxis and ferries can get you almost anywhere in the city. Taxis, rideshares and rental cars can be helpful when traveling further distances, zipping quickly from door-to-door, or to specific out-of-the-way attractions.

Light Rail

The light rail is great for big-picture Seattle travel. There are two lines – line 1, which focuses on Seattle proper, and the newly opened line 2, which winds its way up and down the Eastside. Most visitors will only need to use line 1. It's also the most cost-effective way to travel from the airport to just about anywhere in Seattle proper – and during peak traffic hours, it may even be faster than a taxi or rideshare.

Bus

If the light rail can't get you exactly where you want to go, there's a very good chance that the public bus system will be able to do so. Buses are great for neighborhoods that aren't along the light rail's line – think Magnolia or Ballard, for example. There's also a particularly speedy bus – the G Line – that runs directly from Capitol Hill to Down-town Seattle and often comes in handy.

ESSENTIAL APP

The Transit Go app allows you to plan your routes and purchase your tickets.

Monorail

There's just one monorail line – with just two stops – in Seattle, but it's particularly convenient for visitors. Running from downtown's Westlake Center to Seattle Center, it unites two of the main tourist hubs in the city. Even better, you get a pretty awesome, up-close view of the amorphous MoPOP building as the monorail squeezes through.

Streetcars

There are two streetcar lines in the city. The first runs from Belltown, through South Lake Union and into East Lake Union. The second runs from Pioneer Square, through the International District and First Hill, and into Capitol Hill. While cute and handy when carrying a bunch of items, the streetcars run just as fast as the average walker.

Water Taxi

The water taxi runs from downtown Seattle to West Seattle. While you can travel between the two via other modes of transportation, the 15-minute sail is by far the most fun.

Ferry

Other than the water taxis, you'll find larger ferries crossing Puget Sound on a regular basis. There are numerous ferries connecting the land on either side of this body of water, as well as the islands within, but Bainbridge Island is the most popular destination for Seattle travelers. The ferries often don't run on time, so be sure to give yourself a bit of buffer.

Taxis & Rideshares

At the end of the day, Seattle public transportation can get a little convoluted, depending on your start and end points. For easy door-to-door transportation, there's always the option to get around via taxi or rideshare. These modes of transportation are also great when Seattle weather isn't the most accommodating.

Public Transport Essentials

Despite the many types of public transportation, the payment method options are much more straightforward.

ORCA Card

An ORCA card is the most popular way to pay for transit in Seattle. It works on all modes of transportation, so it's an absolute breeze. You can buy an ORCA card at just about every light rail station via a designated ORCA vending machine. It's $3 to purchase, then you'll load up the balance to cover the cost of all your transportation needs. You can add money to your card at these same vending machines or on the convenient myORCA app. Finally, you can use either a physical card or an electronic one stored in your phone's digital wallet. Just scan either at the dedicated scanners at each transportation location.

Transit Go App

If you want to skip the vending machines and save the $3 of an ORCA card, you can use the Transit Go app. The downside, though, is that Transit Go doesn't work on all types of transportation (the monorail and certain ferries are excluded).

Cash & Card

If neither the ORCA card nor the Transit Go app appeals to you, you can go old-school. Find ticket machines at every necessary light rail, streetcar, water taxi and ferry stop. For buses, you can pay the driver in cash – though they don't have change.

DRIVING & PARKING

If you choose to drive, the PayByPhone app can make paying for parking easier (though it doesn't help with finding parking).

TICKETS

The table below features prices for one adult. There are often discounts for those aged 65+, and kids can usually ride for free.

	Single Journey	Day Pass
Light rail	$3	$6
Street car	$2.25	$4.50
Monorail	$4	n/a
Bus (King County Metro)	$2.75	$6
Water Taxi (to West Seattle)	$5.75	n/a
Ferry (passenger rate)	$10.25	n/a

A Few Surprises

Decades-forgotten relics, mythical creature signage, and speakeasy-esque businesses are just a few of the surprises tucked away in Seattle.

Relics of Seattle Past

With all of the towering glass skyscrapers and modern tech companies, Seattle very much feels like a city of all things new. In reality, the city was incorporated back in 1865, and relics of decades past are still dotted around.

In the International District, the decommissioned **Union Station** (p61) sits among loads of other brick buildings, and each day thousands of people pass on by without ever knowing about the beaux-arts-style Great Hall inside.

In neighboring Pioneer Square – the oldest part of Seattle – the first iteration of the city is sunken and hidden below your feet in the Seattle **underground** (p63). The many black wrought-iron stairways lead to the depths of the old city streets and weathered storefronts – though most, if not all, are private property,

so explore with a tour. There are even clusters of small, square skylights in the sidewalks, hinting at the abandoned remnants below.

Sasquatch Crossing

Washington State has the most reported Bigfoot sightings anywhere in the world. This maybe-not-so-mythical sasquatch has made its mark on the state's outdoor spaces, with 'Sasquatch Crossing' signs and stickers popping up sporadically. Keep your eyes out for these fun, bright yellow signs in places like **Discovery Park** (p94), **Seward Park** (p128) and **Lincoln Park** (p139).

Businesses in Businesses

Things aren't always quite as they seem with Seattle businesses, with quite a few housing hidden (legal) operations – open to the public, if you know where to find them.

OFFBEAT SEATTLE

Take a tour of the decommissioned **Georgetown Steam Plant** (p128) for an almost movie-esque step back in time.

Watch the sunset amid the rusty ruins of a former gasification plant at **Gas Works Park** (p116).

Admire old-school printing machinery – and the art, cards and note-books made on them – at **Day Moon Press** (p131).

Sail away on Lake Union in style on a bubbling **Hot Tub Boat** (p94).

Gas Works Park (p116)

Pop into **Hometeam** (p69), an Italian restaurant with some of the coolest sneakers around; find the speakeasy-esque **Phocific Standard Time** (p87) tucked above an unassuming Vietnamese eatery; or dress up for a dinner at the **Peasant** (p119), a high-end eatery hidden inside the Beast and Cleaver butcher shop.

Revamped Alleyways

With Puget Sound on one side and Lake Washington on the other, Seattle has limited land, so the city has learned to make use of every nook and cranny – and alley. Take **Post Alley** (p46), for instance – once a utilitarian backstreet for postal workers, it's now brimming with shops and restaurants. More recently, the **Belltown Corridor** (p75) has undergone its own transformation, blossoming from an overlooked sidestreet to a mural-filled art walk. Even places that have never been an alley embrace the cleverly utilized mentality, like the high-end **Off Alley** (p130) restaurant, where diners savor an eight-course $200+ tasting menu in a 12-person space reminiscent of a cozy brick hallway.

Literary Nuggets

Beyond the funky bookstores, like Ballard's cookbook-filled **Book Larder** (p121) and architecture-focused **Peter Miller Books** (p69) in Pioneer Square, there are more literary gems dotted throughout the city. Find indie publishing houses tucked in the most unexpected places, or book quotes as mural centerpieces or scribbled on coffee-shop chalkboards.

37

Explore Seattle

Ballard Locks (p114)
GEORGECOLEPHOTO/SHUTTERSTOCK

See p51
for eating,
drinking and
shopping
listings

Explore
Pike Place Market & Downtown

In pre-pandemic times, the tall buildings that make up Downtown Seattle were filled with office workers and the streets were bustling with cars, retail stores and foot traffic. These days it's slowly coming back, thanks to initiatives such as Seattle Restored, a city-funded program that activates empty storefronts with retail pop-ups and art installations from local entrepreneurs, artists and manufacturers in an effort to reinvigorate the area. Beyond the boxy skyscrapers, the city is given welcome oomph by the new-and-improved Waterfront Overlook Walk and Pike Place Market, the city's heart, soul and number-one must-see sight.

Getting Around

 Light Rail
It's best to get around using the two Link light rail stops: Westlake and Symphony.

 On Foot
The area is roughly around 1.5 sq miles, which means there isn't a whole lot of ground to cover, making walking a great option for many. Do note that many streets and sidewalks in the Downtown area are quite steep.

 Rideshares
Rideshares work as a great alternative to walking. They're readily available and enable you to avoid the difficulties – and hefty prices – of parking.

Seattle Great Wheel (p45)
SARAH JANEJ/SHUTTERSTOCK

THE BEST

LOCAL BUSINESS-FILLED MARKET
Pike Place Market (p46)

KID-FRIENDLY ACTIVITY
Seattle Aquarium (p45)

OYSTERS ON THE HALF SHELL
Oyster Cellar (p52)

MODERN COFFEE SHOP
FUTUREBEAN by Storyville Coffee (p52)

NATIVE-OWNED BOUTIQUE
Eighth Generation (p53)

A **B** **C** **D**

1

❶ *Seattle Free Walking Tours*

Hellenika Cultured Creamery

⑦

Seattle Dumpling Co

⑩

Piroshky Piroshky

Victor Steinbrueck Park

2

Starbucks

❽

28

Beecher's Handmade Cheese

Crafts & Farmers Market

Pike Place Chowder

Puget Sound Cider Company

⑬

Pike Place Market

25

12

Woodring Northwest Specialties

Bite Society Cookies

⑨

Public Market Center Sign

Market Parking 🅿

23

Pasta Casalinga

Golden Age Collectables

Pike Place Fish Market

⑭

26

3

22

29

Gum Wall

⑪

Post Alley

Piers 59 & 60

30

31

⑯

Seattle Art Museum ❸

4

THE WATERFRONT

21

Elliott Bay

Pier 57

University St

5

For more see

Top Experiences ⭐ p46
Experiences 🔴 p50
Eating 🟢 p51
Drinking 🔵 p52
Shopping 🟣 p53

Pier 56

Pier 55

6

Ⓝ 0 ⸺⸺⸺ 200 m
0 ⸺⸺⸺ 0.1 miles

Pier 54

A **B** **C** **D**

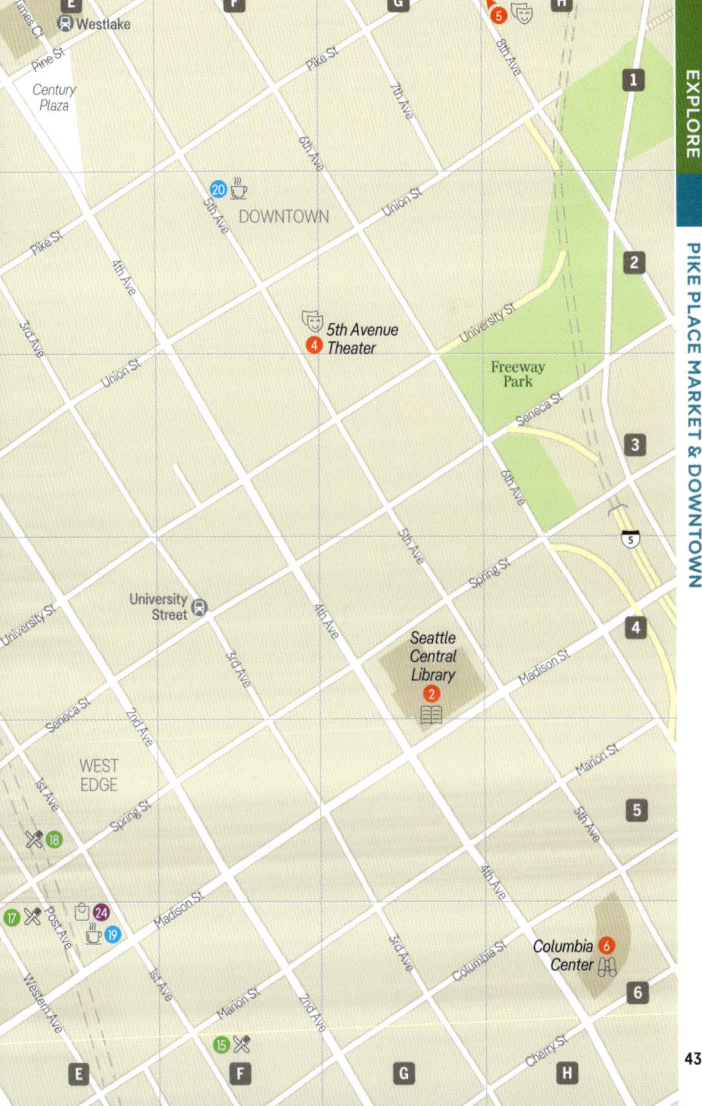

E F G H

1

5

E Westlake

Century
Plaza

Pine St

Times Sq

Pike St

7th Ave

6th Ave

8th Ave

20

DOWNTOWN

5th Ave

Union St

2

5th Avenue
4 **Theater**

Pike St

4th Ave

3rd Ave

Union St

University St

6th Ave

Freeway
Park

Seneca St

3

5

University
Street

University St

3rd Ave

4th Ave

5th Ave

Spring St

Seattle
Central
Library
2

Madison St

Spring St

4

WEST
EDGE

18

1st Ave

Spring St

Madison St

Marion St

5th Ave

5

17

24

19

Post Ave

Madison St

4th Ave

3rd Ave

2nd Ave

Marion St

Columbia St

Columbia
Center **6**

6

Western Ave

Marion St

15

2nd Ave

3rd Ave

Cherry St

1st Ave

E F G H

 **WALKING TOUR**

The Best of the Waterfront

So much of the beauty of Seattle comes from its location on Puget Sound, a stunning network of saltwater inlets and islands that sparkles under the summer sun. Enjoy some of the best views of this waterway with a stroll along the Seattle waterfront, where aquariums, Ferris wheels, quirky shops and unending views await.

START	END	LENGTH
Seattle Overlook Walk	Ye Olde Curiosity Shop	0.6 miles; 30min

① The New & Improved Waterfront

Opened in late 2024, the sparkly new **Overlook Walk** has revitalized the city's waterfront area. It's now easier than ever to get from Pike Place Market to views of Puget Sound. Even better, the area is dotted with benches, tables and green spaces, perfect for a makeshift picnic with unbeatable views.

② 10,000 Marine Animals

More than 10,000 underwater creatures call the **Seattle Aquarium** *(seattleaquarium.org; adult/child from $34/22)* home. Within its tanks, you'll find otters and seahorses, rays and sharks, and even a Giant Pacific octopus. Most recently, the aquarium has added a state-of-the-art Ocean Pavilion, which includes a 360,000-gallon tank housing numerous sea animals from the Indo-Pacific region. Even without an entry ticket, you can peek inside this new section through the large window at the front of the aquarium.

③ Up & Away

The 175ft **Seattle Great Wheel** *(seattlegreatwheel.com; adult/child $23/18)* was installed in June 2012 with 42 gondolas, each capable of carrying eight people on a 12-minute ride. The now-iconic Ferris wheel sticks out over the water on Pier 57 and has quickly become synonymous with Seattle's ever-improving waterfront. On weekend nights, the wheel puts on a light show using 50,000 LED lights.

④ A Native Art Showcase

Just off the waterfront walkway lies **Tidelands** *(thisistidelands.com)*, a gallery dedicated to Indigenous art and storytelling. Peruse the captivating photographs, settle in for a poetry reading, or listen to a musical performance. There's even a small boutique of Native-inspired and -created wares, including clothing, pottery and jewelry.

⑤ Sailing the Seattle Harbor

After strolling along beautiful Puget Sound, it's only natural to want to sail on it. Luckily, the locally owned **Argosy Cruises** *(argosycruises.com; adult/child, $45/29)* has several daily cruises departing from the Seattle waterfront's Pier 55 that do just that. Its popular Harbor Cruise is one hour of delightfully informative narration and lovely city-skyline views. If the weather is clear enough, you may be able to see all the way to Mt Rainier (p154).

⑥ Quirky & Kitschy

Opened in 1899, **Ye Olde Curiosity Shop** *(yeoldecuriosityshop.com)* has long been a Seattle institution. In this part souvenir shop, part museum, you can expect to find things like shrunken heads and mummies alongside Native American art and a plethora of affordable oddities and gifts.

⭐ **TOP EXPERIENCE**

Pike Place Market

A cavalcade of noise, smells, quirkiness and personalities sprinkled liberally around a spatially challenged waterside strip, Pike Place Market is a quintessential Seattle attraction. In operation since 1907 and still as soulful today as it was on day one, this wonderfully local experience highlights the city for what it really is: all-embracing, eclectic and proudly unique.

MAP P42 **C2**

PLANNING TIP
As one of the top attractions in Seattle, Pike Place Market is often very busy. To avoid the crowds, visit as close to the 7am opening as possible and ideally no later than 10am.

Use the official map to navigate this maze-like attraction.

The Iconic Attractions

Walking to Pike Place Market via Pike St, you simply can't miss the huge **Public Market Center sign** etched against the horizon. Incidentally, the sign and clock, installed in 1927, constituted one of the first pieces of outdoor neon on the West Coast.

Just below the sign at the main entryway to the market, you'll find the famed fishmongers at **Pike Place Fish Market**, tossing 10+-pound salmon through the air. You may have to stick around for a bit to see the fish throwing in action, but it often happens when someone orders a fish or is celebrating a special occasion.

From the entryway sign and the salmon tossers below, it's a short walk to **Post Alley**. Named for its hitching posts, this narrow alleyway is lined with shops and restaurants. Add the brick walls and twinkle lights to the mix, and it feels a world away from the tech buildings of Seattle, with a bit of a New England or European feel to it. At the southern end of Post Alley, you'll find the famed **Gum Wall**, Seattle's oddest and most unhygienic sight. The once-venerable red-brick facade is now covered in used pieces of chewing gum, originally

ADELE HEIDENREICH/SHUTTERSTOCK

stuck there by bored theatergoers standing in line for a nearby ticket office in the 1990s. Despite early attempts by the city council to sanitize, the gum-stickers persevered and in 1999, the wall was declared a tourist attraction. Feel free to add your own well-chewed morsels to the Jackson Pollock–like display.

Food & Drink Finds

One of the best ways to explore Pike Place Market is by simply wandering around and seeing what you stumble upon. After all, there are hundreds of vendors selling their finely crafted wares; one visitor will be intrigued by a completely different set of sellers than the next.

With food and drinks alone, there's an endless list waiting to be explored. There are several sit-down spots, like the tucked-away **Seattle**

TAKE A BREAK
Without question, Starbucks is the most iconic coffee spot in Pike Place Market. Though not the original location – that building was torn down – it's the longest standing one. Be prepared to stand in a lengthy line.

NO BIG BUSINESS
A market law prohibits chain stores and ensures all businesses are locally owned. The one exception is Starbucks, which gets away with its market location because it's the coffee giant's first outlet.

Dumpling Co, with its delicate soup dumplings, and **Pasta Casalinga**, known for its comforting homemade pasta. Then there are the beloved grab-and-go eateries – snag a cup of clam chowder from **Pike Place Chowder**, an underrated kimchi grilled cheese from **Beecher's Handmade Cheese**, or a filled-and-fried piroshki from the aptly named **Piroshky Piroshky**, just to start.

In the mood for something sweet? You've got options, both to enjoy on the spot or to pack away for later. Stock up on tayberry jam from **Woodring Northwest Specialties**, buttery **Bite Society Cookies** and chocolate-covered **Chukar Cherries**, or treat yourself in the moment to arguably the best marionberry frozen yogurt around from **Hellenika Cultured Creamery**.

EASTANDWEST/SHUTTERSTOCK

The market also has a few noteworthy drink vendors, including the honey-infused creations of **Hierophant Meadery** (weekends only) and the crisp ciders from **Puget Sound Cider Company** (weekends only). These two are usually scattered throughout the more temporary-looking booths, rather than the brick-and-mortar spaces.

At the end of it all, gather up your goodies for a makeshift picnic of sorts. Enjoy it at the nearby Overlook Walk (p45) or **Victor Steinbrueck Park** under the Seattle summer sunshine. (It's important to note that it's illegal to consume alcohol in public in Seattle, so save those drinks for another time).

Blooming Bouquets

No trip to Pike Place Market would be complete without admiring the dozens of stands selling blooming bouquets. Most of the flower vendors are found on the main level, near enough to the neon Pike Place Market sign, so they're hard to miss. Depending on the season, they'll be selling bouquets with everything from local tulips to daffodils to cherry blossoms.

Unique Shopping

Amid the food nooks and flower vendors, there are quite a few unique shopping experiences to be had in the hustle and bustle of Pike Place Market. Stock up your library at **Lamplight Books**, or fill your shelves with vintage comics and original movie scripts from **Golden Age Collectables** instead. Support local creatives at the **Crafts & Farmers Market**, found on the main level of the market near the Stewart St intersection, or splurge on the most incredible leather creations at **Leolo Handmade Shoes & Leather Goods**, tucked away in the southernmost section of the market.

THE ORIGINS OF THE MARKET
Pike Place Market is the oldest continuously operating market in the nation. It was established in 1907 to give local farmers a place to sell their fruit and vegetables and bypass the middleman. Soon, the greengrocers made room for fishmongers, bakers, butchers, cheese sellers and purveyors of the rest of the Northwest's agricultural bounty. The market's heyday was in the 1930s.

EXPERIENCES

Take One of the Seattle Free Walking Tours

TOUR

MAP: **1** P42 **A1**

Seattle Free Walking Tours (*seattlefreetours.com*) offers an intimate two-hour walk taking in Pike Place Market, the waterfront and Pioneer Sq, among other tours. Each tour is 'pay what you can', and the company notes that comparable walking tours run around $25. Reserve online.

Pop by the Seattle Central Library

LIBRARY

MAP: **2** P42 **G4**

Rivaling the Space Needle (p76) and the Museum of Pop Culture (p80) for architectural ingenuity, **Seattle Central Library** (*spl.org/hours-and-locations/central-library*) is a spectacle of glass, curves and edges. This $165.5-million sculpture of glass and steel holds over a million books, along with a slew of facilities, including a map room, music practice rooms and an aptly named (though a bit tricky to find) 'red floor'. Come here to enjoy art, architecture and literary comfort.

Spend a Few Hours at the Seattle Art Museum

MUSEUM

MAP: **3** P42 **D4**

The collection at the **Seattle Art Museum** (*SAM; seattleart museum.org; adult/child from*

$30/free) feels uncommon, intimate and extraordinary. Its sterling selection of contemporary and antique art of the Indigenous peoples of the Pacific Northwest alone makes this a required stop on any visit to the Emerald City.

Catch an Evening Show

NIGHTLIFE

Downtown Seattle is home to two of the best live-performance venues in the city: the **5th Avenue Theater** (MAP: **4** P42 **F2**; *5thavenue. org*) and the **Paramount Theater** (MAP: **5** P42 **H1**; *paramounttheatre seattle.net*). The former is renowned for its Broadway-caliber musicals, while the latter is an opulent historic landmark that hosts everything from concerts to theatrical productions.

Take in the Views from the Columbia Center

VIEWPOINT

MAP: **6** P42 **H6**

Everyone rushes for the iconic Space Needle, when the sleek 932ft **Columbia Center** (*columbia centerseattle.com; adult/child $25/19*) is really the tallest Seattle viewpoint. Take the elevators up to the plush Sky View Observatory on the 73rd floor, from where you can look down on ferries, cars, islands and – ha, ha – the Space Needle!

Best Places for...

$** Budget **$$** Midrange **$$$ Top End

See p42 for map of locations

Eating

Savory Finds in Pike Place Market

Pink Door **$$$**

7 B2

A restaurant like no other, the Pink Door is probably the only place in the world where you can enjoy fabulous linguine *alle vongole* (pasta with clams and pancetta) while watching live jazz, burlesque cabaret or – we kid you not – a trapeze artist swinging from the 20ft ceiling. *11:30am-10pm Tue-Sat*

Café Campagne **$$$**

8 C2

Inside Café Campagne's effortlessly elegant interior, live vicariously as a French poseur over steamed mussels, hanger steaks, generous portions of frites and crispy vegetables. Save room for the crème brûlée dessert. Love it? Return for weekend brunch. *9am-9pm Mon-Fri, 8am-9pm Sat, 8am-8pm Sun*

Matt's in the Market **$$$**

9 C3

Matt's, now run by a former Pike Place Market fish-thrower, is perched above the bustle of the market. Most of the ingredients on the menu come from down below. Expect plenty of fish, fresh veg and organic meats. *11:30am-2:30pm, plus 5:30-10pm Mon-Sat*

Maíz **$$**

10 B2

Get your Mexican food fix at Maíz, where the tamales, chilaquiles and tacos are sure to please. *11am-3pm Mon-Fri, 11am-1:30pm Sat & Sun, plus 5-9:30pm Thu-Sun*

Sweet Bites in Pike Place Market

Freya Bakery & Cafe **$**

11 C3

Flaky pastries are the name of the game at Freya Bakery & Cafe. Go for a traditional croissant, or opt for the Scandinavian *kardemommesnurrer* (cardamom knot) or the churro cruffin if you're in the mood for something different. *8am-4pm*

Crumpet Shop **$**

12 C3

A little hole-in-the-wall that has been around for decades, the Crumpet Shop freshly makes its subtle, soft crumpets and tops them with set accompaniments – think raspberry preserves and ricotta or pesto, tomato and parmesan. *7am-4pm*

A Morning Treat

Ben Paris **$**

13 D2

Though also open for dinner, weekday breakfast and weekend brunch are the stars of the show at this modern American restaurant (even with the brief four-item breakfast menu). Don't miss the vanilla bean anglaise-topped ricotta pancakes. *hours vary*

Baxter & Frost ⑤
 14 D3

Before you even see Baxter & Frost's storefront, you'll smell the intoxicating scent of baked goods wafting down the street. Whether you're craving fluffy cinnamon rolls, mini raspberry pies or classic chocolate chip cookies to start your day, they'll have it here. *10am-8pm Mon-Thu, to 9pm Fri-Sun*

Seafood at its Finest

Oyster Cellar ⑤⑤⑤
15 F6

As its name implies, the Oyster Cellar specializes in two things: fresh, shucked oysters and impeccably crafted cocktails. Visit during happy hour *(3-6pm Tue-Sat)* for oysters at $2 a pop. *3-9pm Tue-Sat*

MARKET Seafood Eatery ⑤⑤
16 D4

It can be hard to find casual yet well-made seafood, but MARKET Seafood Eatery delivers. Try the hot Connecticut lobster roll or the PNW crab roll from this Downtown spot. *10am-6pm Wed & Fri-Sun, to 8pm Thu*

International Eats

Skalka ⑤
17 E6

Showcasing *khachapuri*, a traditional pizza-esque dish from the country of Georgia, this self-serve eatery offers a wonderful introduction to South Caucasus cuisine. *9am-7pm*

Mint Progressive Indian ⑤⑤⑤
18 E5

Mint isn't your typical Indian restaurant. Find fun twists like the bone-in *pompano kafreal* (masala-marinated fried fish) and modernist nitrogen *chaat* (savory, crunchy snack), prepared tableside. Pair your meal with one of its beyond-creative cocktails. *11am-9:30pm*

Drinking

Modern Coffee Shops

FUTUREBEAN by Storyville Coffee
19 E6

The Downtown location of this cozy yet modern coffee shop serves impeccable breakfast sandwiches, cinnamon rolls, salted caramel cookies and, of course, coffee. *8am-2pm*

Olympia Coffee Roasting
20 F2

With soaring ceilings, large windows and comfortable seating, Olympia Coffee Roasting is an incredible spot to sip a cup of coffee. *6am-6pm Mon-Fri, 7am-6pm Sat & Sun*

Local Brews & Booze

Locust Cider
21 D4

Tucked in Post Alley, this family-owned cider nook is known for its refreshing ciders and retro video games. *2-10pm Mon-Thu, 11am-10pm Fri & Sat, 11am-8pm Sun*

Zig Zag Café
22 B3

Zig Zag Café repopularized the gin-based Jazz Age cocktail 'The Last Word' in the early 2000s. The drink went viral and the bar's nattily attired mixers were rightly hailed as the city's finest alchemists. *5pm-midnight*

Shopping

For Your Kitchen

DeLaurenti Food & Wine

23 C3

A Pike Place Market veteran, this Italian grocery store–deli has been run by the same family since 1946. It offers a beautifully old-fashioned selection of wine, cheese and sausages, along with a large range of capers, olive oils and anchovies. *9am-5pm*

For Your Walls

Michael Birawar Gallery

24 E6

Michael Birawar is known for painting urban landscapes – in this case, Seattle – in a sort of trippy, surrealist manner. Admire his works, alongside those of other acclaimed artists, at this Downtown gallery. *10am-5pm*

Metsker Maps

25 C3

This nearly century-old shop is all about maps –

historic and modern, in globe-form or in puzzle-form, of fictional lands or of the starry night sky. *9am-6pm Mon-Fri, 10am-6pm Sat & Sun*

For Your Closet

Eighth Generation

26 D3

Home to 100% Native-designed products and owned by the Snoqualmie Tribe, Eighth Generation boasts an incredible collection of patterned blankets, nature-inspired jewelry, brightly colored socks and more. *10am-5pm Wed-Sun*

Zebraclub

27 B2

This Pike Place Market shop stocks trendy clothing and accessories from hard-to-find brands, including OBEY, Dark Seas and Kuwalla. *10am-4:45pm Fri-Tue*

Pendleton

28 C2

Rooted in the Pacific Northwest, Pendleton crafts premium wool blankets, flannels and more, using some of the finest wool available. *11am-6pm*

For Your Home

pirkko. Finland

29 D3

This Scandinavian-inspired homewares store stocks everything from calm, nature-inspired dinnerware sets to neon Isle Jacobsen rain jackets. *11am-5pm Mon-Sat, to 4pm Sun*

Seattle Antiques Market

30 C4

The Seattle Antiques Market is a sprawling marketplace brimming with vintage finds from bygone eras. From ornate furniture to curious nautical artifacts, it's a fantastic place to hunt for storied treasures and unique additions to your collection. *10am-6pm*

Seattle Waterfront Marketplace

31 C4

A collective of over 50 artists, the relatively under-the-radar Seattle Waterfront Marketplace is filled with watercolor paintings and handmade mugs, floral soaps and artsy planners. It's great for one-of-a-kind gifts and souvenirs. *noon-5pm*

Bainbridge Island

Take a beautiful 35-minute ferry ride from Downtown Seattle and across Puget Sound to Bainbridge Island. It's the charm of a small town, the beauty of an outdoorsy waterfront destination, and the food scene of a big city suburb all wrapped into one incredible location.

GETTING THERE

To get to Bainbridge Island, take a ferry from Downtown Seattle across Puget Sound. Get to the ferry terminal early – especially if you're taking a car – as the ferries can fill up. If you don't make it on, you'll have to wait about 40 minutes for the next one.

Scan for the Seattle–Bainbridge ferry schedule.

The Port Area

From the ferry terminal, it's about a five-minute walk to the start of the action. Pop into numerous museums, including the **Bainbridge Island Historical Museum** *(bainbridgehistory museum.org)* and the **Bainbridge Island Museum of Art** *(biartmuseum.org)*, as well as a few of the attention-grabbing shops along the main throughway, like the whimsical **Bainbridge Apothecary and Tea Shop** *(bainbridgeapothecaryandteashop.com)* and the trendy home-goods store **Salt House Mercantile**.

Ready for a bite to eat? **Proper Fish** *(properfish.com)* may very well whip up the best British-style fish and chips in greater Seattle, while Vietnamese **Ba Sa** *(basabainbridgeisland. com)* will have you wanting to sail back to the island just for another bite. Even the well-located **Town & Country** *(townandcountry markets.com/markets/bainbridge)* grocery store is worth a stop for fresh Seattle favorites, like marionberry gelato and house-made smoked salmon spread, along with grab-and-go eats. Before you ferry back to the city, stop into **Bainbridge Brewing Alehouse** *(bainbridgebeer.com)* for an ice-cold beer, brewed right on this laid-back island.

OKSANA.PERKINS/SHUTTERSTOCK

Greater Bainbridge Island

If you choose to bring a car across the Sound or hitch a ride on the public buses, you can explore the rest of Bainbridge Island, which, for the most part, has stayed off visitors' radars. Wander the peaceful **Bloedel Reserve** *(bloedelreserve.org; adult/child $22/5)*: 150 acres of towering trees and manicured landscapes makes for a wonderful stroll or picnic spot.

Looking for lunch? Drive to **Via Rosa 11** *(viarosa11.com)*, an unassuming restaurant serving arguably the best Italian food in the greater Seattle area. Everything is hand-made – from the fresh pastas to the soon-to-be-wood-fired pizza dough.

TAKE A BREAK
Pegasus
Coffee House
(pegasuscoffee. com) is a Bainbridge staple, serving up excellent coffee drinks and pastries since 1980. Lines can get long after each ferry docking, so try to time your coffee stop between the rushes.

See p66
for eating,
drinking and
shopping
listings

中華門

Explore
Pioneer Square, International District & SoDo

It's easy enough to cross between the three back-to-back Seattle neighborhoods of Pioneer Square, the International District and SoDo during a leisurely stroll around the city. But despite the close proximity, each has a distinct atmosphere that makes it relatively easy to notice when you move from one to another. Pioneer Square is historic and almost grungy; the International District celebrates global cultures through its restaurants, shops and dragon-entwined light poles; and SoDo is an intriguing combination of industrial and sporty and is marked by two iconic sports venues – Lumen Field and T-Mobile Park.

Getting Around

 Light Rail
There are four light rail stops: Pioneer Square Station, Int'l District/Chinatown Station, Stadium Station and SoDo Station.

On Foot
When you've reached your light rail stop, it's often easy enough to get around on foot, though there are some very steep streets.

Bus & Streetcar
If the roads are a bit too steep, buses and the First Hill Streetcar are both great intra-neighborhood transportation options.

Historic Chinatown Gate (p61)
MELISSA HERZOG/SHUTTERSTOCK

★
THE BEST

ARCHITECTURAL GEM
Union Station (p61)

CUTESY GIFT SHOP
Sairen (p68)

MODERN FILIPINO BITES
Hood Famous Cafe + Bar (p68)

FORTUNE COOKIE SPOT
Tsue Chong Retail Store (p69)

HISTORIC TOUR
Seattle Underground Tour (p63)

Beneath the Streets

Bill Speidel's Underground Tour

Smith Tower

Pioneer Square

PIONEER SQUARE

Waterfall Garden

Occidental Square

Klondike Gold Rush National Historical Park

Occidental Mall

King St Station (Amtrak)

Union Station

PIONEER SQUARE

Lumen Field

Columbia St
1st Ave
Post Ave
Western Ave
Cherry St
2nd Ave
James St
3rd Ave
Jefferson St
5th Ave
Alaskan Way
Yesler Way
SR99
S Washington St
2nd Ave Ext S
Prefontaine Pl S
4th Ave
S Main St
Nord Al
Occidental Ave S
S Jackson St
1st Ave S
Occidental Ave S
S King St
4th Ave S
Sth Dearborn St
SR99
Alaskan Way S
1st Ave S

E F G H

Harborview
Park

FIRST
HILL

Broadway

8th Ave

6th Ave

5

1

Yesler Way

Yesler
Terrace

5th Ave S

6th Ave S

S Washington St

2

JAPANTOWN

Kobe
Terrace
Park

S Main St

21

20

5th & Jackson/
Japantown

18

40

23

7th & Jackson/
Chinatown

17

26

27

3

S Jackson St

Maynard Ave S

S Jackson St

Canton Al S

8th Ave S

10th Ave S

54

International
District/
Chinatown

Hing Hay
Park

14

24

7th Ave S

25

13

15

34

S King St

22

S King St

S King St

59

42

16

Seattle
Pinball
Museum

4

CHINATOWN

**Wing Luke
Museum**

52

INTERNATIONAL
DISTRICT

S Weller St

S Weller St

19

35

5th Ave S

6th Ave S

53

58

Maynard Ave S

7th Ave S

S Lane St

S Lane St

12 *Kilig*

5

Airport Way S

S Dearborn St

8th Ave S

For more see

Top Experiences ⭐ p62
Experiences 🌸 p63
Eating 🌿 p66
Drinking 🍷 p67
Shopping 🛍 p68

5

90

S Charles St

6

N
0 ————— 200 m
0 ————— 0.1 miles

Airport Way S

E F G H

WALKING TOUR

The Heart of the International District

There are technically three official sub-neighborhoods that call this area home – Chinatown, Japantown and Little Saigon. The first two are the easiest to access and are woven into each other, making them the perfect pair to explore on foot.

START	END	LENGTH
King Street Station	Panama Hotel Tea & Coffee House	0.5 miles; 1hr

1 The Gateway to Seattle

Welcoming visitors via Amtrak train from Vancouver, Los Angeles and even as far as Chicago, **King Street Station** is an architectural sight to behold. On the outside, admire the soaring red-brick clock tower, reminiscent of the landmark one in Venice's St Mark's Sq. On the inside, ornate beaux-arts-style details come to life through intricate plasterwork, evoking a sense of timeless elegance.

2 A European-Style Architectural Marvel

Just across the street, tucked among the light-rail entry points, you'll find the decommissioned but still stunning **Union Station**. Often overlooked and mistaken for the still-active King Street Station, Union Station is an architectural gem all on its own. The red-brick exterior hides the barrel-vaulted Great Hall, adorned with intricate beaux-arts-style carvings, thoughtfully placed light fixtures and a few skylights.

3 The Entryway to Chinatown

Upon exiting Union Station, you'll see the **Historic Chinatown Gate**. Built in 2007 and dedicated in 2008, this modern Paifang archway was built to mark the west entrance to the Chinatown neighborhood and celebrate the vibrant Chinese community in the area.

4 A Park of Culture

Heading east on King St, you'll hit **Hing Hay Park** (*seattle.gov/ parks/allparks/hing-hay-park*)

and the Grand Pavilion. Welcoming visitors with traditional Chinese architecture and community events, it serves as a focal point and hub of the neighborhood. Even when there's no particular event happening, you'll still likely find some local community members playing friendly games of ping pong and chess.

5 A Historic Japanese American Hub

Originally known as the Higo Ten-Cent Store and now as **Kobo Shop & Gallery at HIGO** (*koboseattle. com*), this retail space has long served as a community hub for the Japanese American community, first at its original 1909 Weller St location, then at its current location since 1932. Today, the shop has artifacts and memorabilia from the previous store, along with new art pieces from contemporary Japanese and PNW artists.

6 The Last Tea House of its Kind

At the opposite side of the block (and up a steep hill) lies the **Panama Hotel Tea & Coffee House** (*panamahotelseattle.net/ panama-tea-coffee*). You'll feel transported back in time while sipping tea in this National Treasure–designated 1910 building. It also contains the only remaining Japanese bathhouse in the US (though it's not open for use) and doubles as a memorial to the neighborhood's Japanese residents forced into internment camps during WWII.

⭐ **TOP EXPERIENCE**

Wing Luke Museum

Named after Wing Luke, the first Asian American elected to public office in the Pacific Northwest, the Wing Luke Museum celebrates Asian Pacific American history with exhibits narrating stories of resilience and community contributions.

MAP P58 **G4**

PLANNING TIP
All tickets to the Wing Luke Museum serve as an all-day pass, so you can leave and come back as many times as you'd like.

Ongoing Exhibits

The **Wing Luke Museum** (*wingluke.org; adult/child $17/free*) has a handful of ongoing exhibits, the most popular of which is the one dedicated to prominent martial artist and actor Bruce Lee. Learn more about his philosophy of life, and even get a glimpse of his extensive 2800-book library. Beyond that, there are a few exhibits dedicated to specific ethnicities and the marks they've made on the International District and Seattle as a whole, including the Cambodian Cultural Museum, Hometown Desi, and I Am Filipino. The most impactful exhibit of them all may be Honoring Our Journey, a section all about how immigrants from Asia and the Pacific Islands settled in the US and built the thriving Asian American and Pacific Islanders community.

In-Depth Tours

Learn even more about the International District and its communities through the Wing Luke Museum's free general tours. These offer more insights into the historic buildings in which the museum is held, as well as access to the usually closed-off Yick Fung Co Store. The tours take place multiple times per day on Wednesdays through Sundays. Each tour has a maximum capacity of 15 people and is available on a first-come, first-served basis.

Scan for information on hours, accessibility and more.

Explore Seattle's Hidden City: the Underground   TOUR

Believe it or not, the original 1800s Seattle was built on unstable, sandy ground. Over time those buildings began to sink. Then, when the Great Seattle Fire of 1889 came and decimated a 30-block radius, much of the city needed to be rebuilt. Today, visitors can explore these sunken streets and structures – reminiscent of an abandoned construction site crossed with a Hollywood movie set – through tours like **Bill Speidel's Underground Tour** (MAP: ❶ P58 B1; *undergroundtour.com; adult/child $22/10)* and **Beneath the Streets** (MAP: ❷ P58 B1; *beneath-the-streets. com; adult/child $30/19)*. Mix in a little humor and history and you have a recipe for a fun and educational activity.

Soar to the Top of Smith Tower   VIEWPOINT

MAP: ❸ P58 C1

When it was built in 1914, the 42-story **Smith Tower** *(smithtower. com; from $15)* was the fourth tallest building in the world. Now, it doesn't stand up to the skyscrapers of the rest of the Seattle skyline, but it still offers some incredible city views – often without the crowds of the other sky-high landmarks. Admire the 360-degree views of the city and Puget Sound from the wrap-around deck, enjoy the cocktails and small plates at the speakeasy-inspired bar, and take a seat in the storied 'wishing chair'. The wishing chair is said to have been a gift from China's Empress Dowager Cixi, and legend has it that those who are single and sit in the chair will be married within a year.

Play a Few Games at the Seattle Pinball Museum   MUSEUM

MAP: ❹ P58 F4

Unlike traditional museums, the **Seattle Pinball Museum** *(seattle pinballmuseum.com; adult/child, $23/20)* is a sort of interactive haven that allows visitors to play a vast collection of pinball machines spanning decades, with the oldest playable machine dating back to 1960 and the oldest non-playable ones going all the way back to the 1930s. It's a nostalgic journey through vintage and modern games, and it's a hands-on exploration of gaming history. The museum's mission is to preserve and share the joy of pinball, making it an engaging destination for enthusiasts and casual visitors alike. Admission buys you unlimited games for the day, so feel free to stick around as long as you'd like.

Catch a Game at Lumen Field   SPORTS ARENA

MAP: ❺ P58 C5

While **Lumen Field** *(lumenfield. com)* is most well known as the home of the Seattle Seahawks (NFL), this iconic sports arena also lays claim to the Seattle Reign (NWSL) and the Seattle Sounders

(MLS). Each of these three teams has won multiple titles in its respective sports and divisions. Even better, they boast some of the most enthusiastic fan bases in the country, making catching a game at this SoDo stadium a must. Before you know it, you'll be decked out in team colors – with face paint to match – and roaring your support right alongside them.

Watch the Seattle Mariners at the Retro-Style T-Mobile Park
SPORTS ARENA

With its retro-style design, **T-Mobile Park** (MAP: ⑥ P58 **B6**; *mlb. com/mariners/ballpark*) is one of the best-looking stadiums around. But amid the old-school aesthetics, this sports arena has incredible modern features – like a retractable roof that allows for a real grass field – that create an exceptional experience for Seattle Mariners players and fans alike.

To really round out your day at the stadium, be prepared to eat your way all around it too.

Savor mouthwatering pizza slices from **Moto Pizza** (MAP: ⑦ P58 **B6**), innovative ice-cream flavors from **Salt & Straw** (MAP: ⑧ P58 **B6**), and absurdly topped hot dogs from **Sumo Dog** (MAP: ⑨ P58 **B6**), just to start. The affordable $6 beers sold all throughout the stadium act as the cherry on top. So snag some tickets and as many bites as you can feasibly eat, and watch this classic Seattle team play a great all-American game of baseball.

Take a Break at the Waterfall Garden
GARDEN
MAP: ⑩ P58 **C2**

Tucked amid the red-brick buildings of Pioneer Square lies the hidden **Waterfall Garden** (*pioneersquare. org/businesses/waterfall-garden-park*). Built on the site of the first UPS headquarters (which opened

T-Mobile Park

IAN DEWAR PHOTOGRAPHY/SHUTTERSTOCK

Pioneer Square's large population of unhoused people may give some visitors pause, but it's important to keep in mind that they are citizens of the neighborhood the same as anyone else, and pose no more of a threat than their housed neighbors. One way to contribute to the solution is by buying the weekly newspaper *Real Change*. You'll see vendors, many of them unhoused people, selling it on the street for $2 (vendors buy the paper for $0.60 a copy and keep the profit). The paper, founded in 1994, generates over $1 million a year for homeless causes.

back in 1907), this surprisingly tranquil little 'pocket park' is home to an artificial 22ft waterfall and is a fantastic spot for a little downtime. There are even a couple of small tables, perfect for a midday picnic or snack.

Follow the Golden Rush at the Klondike Gold Rush National Historical Park   MUSEUM

MAP: **11** P58 C3

Run by the US National Park Service, this wonderful **museum** (*nps.gov/klgo/index.htm*) has exhibits, from the 1897 Klondike gold rush, when a Seattle-on-steroids acted as a fueling depot for fortune-seeking prospectors bound for the Yukon in Canada. Even better, it's completely free to visit.

Take Part in a Chinatown-International District Food Walk   FOOD WALK

The Chinatown-International District has some of the best food finds in all of Seattle. While it may be impossible to sample them all, the **Chinatown-International District Food Walks** (*seattle chinatownid.com/experiences/food*

-walk-series) make it possible to try. With dozens of local eateries offering small plates for between $4 and $8, you can savor a whole bunch of bites, from dim sum to banh mi. These tasty events take place on the third Saturdays of June, July and August, as well as on Small Business Saturday in November and around Lunar New Year in January or February.

Dive into Filipino Culture   CULTURE

MAP: **12** P58 G5

While there was once an officially recognized Manilatown or Filipino Town – the latter of which is typically the preferred terminology – in Seattle's International District, those designations have controversially fallen to the wayside, leaving just Chinatown, Japantown and Little Saigon. Despite this, Filipino culture and businesses have continued to thrive. The Wing Luke Museum (p62) has a dedicated 'I Am Filipino' exhibit, while restaurants like **Kilig** and Hood Famous Cafe + Bar (p68) serve up delectable Filipino dishes and drinks, both classic and modernized.

Best Places for...

See p58 for map of locations

EXPLORE

PIONEER SQUARE, INTERNATIONAL DISTRICT & SODO

⑤ Budget ⑤⑤ Midrange ⑤⑤⑤ Top End

Eating

Slurpable Noodle Spots

Szechuan Noodle Bowl ⑤

13 G3

This mom-and-pop casual eatery serves crave-worthy veggie dumplings and possibly the best green-onion pancake in the city. *11:30am-8pm Tue-Sun*

Mike's Noodle House ⑤

14 F3

This cozy, cash-only noodle shop is a haven for Chinese comfort food. Opt for any dish featuring its exceptionally thin egg noodles. *10am-7pm Mon-Fri, to 8pm Sat & Sun*

Phnom Penh Noodle House ⑤⑤

15 H3

This Cambodian restaurant stands out from the rest of the International District, with dishes like the seafood-rich Phnom Penh special rice noodle and the sweet-and-spicy Phnom Penh chicken wings being crowd favorites. *11am-8pm Thu-Tue*

One-Item Specialties

King's Barbecue House ⑤

16 E4

This cash-only, take-out-only establishment has mastered the art of roasted duck. If the hanging ducks don't catch your attention, the mouthwatering smell will. *10am-6:30pm*

The Boat ⑤⑤

17 H3

This casual Vietnamese spot specializes in one thing: chicken. Fried and covered in fish sauce and garlicky goodness, it's essentially the only thing on the menu (besides the pandan waffles for dessert). You just choose your sides. *11am-9pm Thu-Tue*

Hot Pot Havens

Chengdu Memory ⑤⑤

18 E3

This Sichuan hot-pot spot has made a name for itself with its punchy flavors and extensive sauce bar. *noon-midnight*

Happy Lamb Hot Pot ⑤⑤

19 F4

Choose your flavorful broth and cook your high-quality meats of choice – lamb belly or wagyu beef, anyone? – at this interactive Mongolian hot-pot chain. *11:30am-11pm*

Japanese Bites

Maneki ⑤⑤

20 E3

For an unforgettable dining experience, reserve one of Maneki's tatami-mat dining rooms (paper and wood lattice private chambers with seating on the floor) and feast on a meal of traditional Japanese cuisine and sake. *5-9pm Tue-Sun*

Onibaba by Tsukushinbo ⑤⑤

21 E3

With no signage (beyond its food safety rating), this Japanese, rice-centered restaurant is a bit secretive. Here, the simple starch is taken to the next level as *onigiri*, *ochazuke* (tea-covered rice), *donburi* (rice bowls) and more. *hours vary*

Fuji Bakery ⑤

22 E4

This corner bakery with Japanese roots prepares baked goods from all around the world – from *ube malasadas* (Hawaii Portuguese donuts) to flaky cruffins. *7:30am-5pm Mon-Sat, to 4pm Sun*

Itsumono

23 F3

Innovative gastropub where Japanese culinary traditions meet international inspiration, offering playful dishes like the tikka tonkatsu udon. *4-10:30pm*

Chinese Restaurants

Kau Kau

24 F4

This casual Chinese nook is all about the meats – specifically its BBQ pork and roasted duck. *10am-8pm Wed-Mon*

Jade Garden

25 G4

Usually mentioned near the top of the list of best places for dim sum in the ID, Jade Garden has a good range of delicacies with everything from steamed pork buns to exotic plates such as chicken's feet. *9am-9pm*

Little Saigon Gems

Phở Bắc Sup Shop

26 H3

This packed restaurant may very well serve up the best pho in the city. Before diving into the heartwarming soup, order a plate of twice-fried chicken wings drizzled in tamarind sauce as an appetizer. *10am-9pm*

Tamarind Tree

27 H3

This legendary, family-owned restaurant has a lengthy menu of Vietnamese

favorites, from duck salad to pho and uber-popular rice cakes (prawn- and pork-filled fried crepes). Don't miss the selection of tropical fruit martinis. *11am-9pm*

Pioneer Square Eats

Mirabelle by Orphée

28 B1

One of the newest editions to the Pioneer Square food scene, this Parisian-inspired cafe and patisserie serves up some of the flakiest, butteriest croissants in the city. *8am-3pm Tue-Fri, to 4pm Sat & Sun*

Salumi Artisan Cured Meats

29 C3

This well-loved deli used to be known for the long lines at its tiny storefront, and although it's moved to a bigger spot, you can still expect a wait for the legendary Italian-quality salami and cured-meat sandwiches. *10am-3pm*

Señor Carbón Restaurant

30 B1

Japanese Peruvian (also known as Nikkei) dishes fill the menu, with flavors like spicy ají amarillo and umami-forward unagi sauce melding together on one plate. Don't forget to get a pisco sour, the national drink of Peru, while you're at it. *noon-9pm Tue-Thu, to 10pm Fri & Sat, to 8pm Sun*

84 Yesler

31 A1

Global influences are the name of the game at this high-end restaurant. Order dishes like seared foie gras and crab-and-herb pappardelle à la carte, or splurge on a four- or six-course tasting menu. *4-9pm Wed-Sat*

Drinking
Cozy Coffee & Tea

Foggy Tea

32 C1

This adorable tea shop specializes in tea lattes – essentially the tea of your choice topped with steamed milk – that are fantastic pick-me-ups. *8:30am-4:30pm Tue & Wed, 10am-5pm Thu-Sat*

Elm Coffee Roasters

33 C2

Get an exceptional cup of joe from Elm Coffee Roasters, one of the only coffee roasters in the neighborhood. *7am-1pm Mon, 7am-3pm Tue-Fri, 10am-2pm Sat*

Phin

34 H3

Named after the traditional Vietnamese coffee brewing tool, Phin is known for its incredible condensed-milk-drizzled Vietnamese coffee. It's also a great spot for *bánh* kẹp (pandan waffles) and *da ua* (homemade Vietnamese yogurt). *8am-3pm Mon & Wed-Fri, to 5pm Sat & Sun*

Hello Em Việt Coffee & Roastery

 35 H4

Personalize your Vietnamese coffee – or *cà phê* – with egg whip, egg cream or milk alternatives at this Little Saigon coffee shop. Grab strawberry-filled mochi clouds (weekends only) and a banh mi while you're at it. *8am-4pm Sun-Fri, to 5pm Sat*

Unique Bar Experiences

Saké Nomi

36 A2

Regardless if you're a sake connoisseur or casual sipper, you're likely to expand your palate and your cultural horizons at this cozy retailer and tasting room in Pioneer Square. *2-8pm Tue-Thu, to 10pm Fri & Sat*

Bad Bishop

37 B1

Craft cocktail bar with upscale American bar bites, like fried Brussels sprouts and harissa-dusted mac 'n' cheese. *4-11pm Tue-Thu, to midnight Fri & Sat*

Spirit Makers

Letterpress Distilling

 38 A6

Specializing in high-quality Italian liqueurs like amaro and limoncello, Letterpress

Distilling is a bit of a hidden gem. Stop into its tasting room for a tasting flight or a well-crafted cocktail. *noon-6pm Sat, to 4pm Sun*

Westland Distillery

39 B6

Settled on SoDo's main thoroughfare, Westland Distillery crafts some of the best whiskey in the city. Visit for a tasting flight, a whiskey-based cocktail, and maybe even a peek at the behind-the-scenes distilling action. *hours vary*

Shopping

Curated Gift Shops

Sairen

40 E3

This thoughtfully curated, Asian-inspired boutique sells the adorable items, like boba-shaped candles, printed tea towels, and punny greeting cards, many of which have been made by local AAPI creatives. *noon-5pm Wed, Thu & Sun, 11am-5pm Fri & Sat*

Flora and Henri

41 B3

Peruse the selection of trendy clothing, chic home-decor items and high-quality skincare products at this Pioneer Square shop. *10am-6pm Mon-Sat, 11am-5pm Sun*

Hood Famous Cafe + Bar

42 E4

Though primarily an eatery, it also has a collection of foodstuffs, stationery and children's books in its entryway. *8am-4pm Tue-Fri, 9am-4pm Sat & Sun*

Old-School Cool

Lander Street Vintage

43 D6

Regarded as one of the best in the city, Lander Street Vintage is a full-on antique mall, with high-end items and quirky home-decor pieces. *noon-6pm Mon-Fri, 11am-6pm Sat & Sun*

Silver Platters

44 C6

This long-established, warehouse-esque record store has one of the largest selections of CDs, vinyl and DVDs in Seattle. *11am-7pm*

Pioneer Square Art Galleries

J Rinehart Gallery

45 C3

With couches and plants dotted throughout the artwork-filled space, it's easy to picture these pieces in your own home. *10am-5pm Tue-Sat*

Greg Kucera Gallery

 46 D2

This art gallery showcases works from local mid-career artists as well as more internationally renowned ones. *10:30am-5:30pm Tue-Sat*

Foster/White Gallery
47 D2

This contemporary art gallery is known for its large-scale paintings and sculptures. *10am-6pm Tue-Sat*

Glasshouse Studio
48 B3

This is the oldest glass-blowing studio in Seattle and has all types of lamps, ornaments, decorative vases and abstract sculptures in its storefront. You may even get to see artists at work. *hours vary*

Cozy Bookstores

Peter Miller Architecture & Design Books
49 A3

This Post Alley bookstore has a bit of a sketchy entrance, but the inside is filled with architecture and design books. *10am-5pm Mon-Sat*

Arundel Books
50 B3

With its ornate archways and ceiling-high bookshelves, Arundel Books feels like it was pulled out of a reader's fairy-tale dreams. *11am-7pm*

Long Brothers Fine & Rare Books
51 C3

The spacious Long Brothers Books is known for its PNW reads and modern, collectable first editions. *10am-6pm Tue & Wed, 10am-8pm Thu-Sat, 11am-6pm Sun*

Retail Food & Drink Finds

Tsue Chong Retail Store
52 G4

Tsue Chong is a major supplier of fortune cookies in Seattle – buy from its small retail store, or opt for the flat, affordable 'unfortunate' cookies that are just as tasty as their shaped counterparts. *7am-3:30pm Mon-Fri, 8am-noon Sat*

Uwajimaya
53 E4

Founded by Fujimatsu Moriguchi, this large department and grocery store – a cornerstone of Seattle's Asian community – has everything from fresh fish to exotic fruits to homewares. *8am-8pm*

New Century Tea Gallery
54 F3

Stock up on dried tea leaves or splurge on a fancy tea set at this Chinatown shop, right next to Hing Hay Park. *11am-5pm Wed-Mon*

A Closet Revamp

Filson
55 B6

Founded in 1897 as the original outfitters for Klondike gold-rush prospectors, Filson is a Seattle legend that, in 2015, opened up this impressive flagship store in SoDo. Wall-mounted bison heads and sepia-toned photos evoke the Klondike spirit. *10am-6pm Mon-Sat, 11am-5pm Sun*

Hometeam
56 C3

You may not expect to discover one of the best sneaker shops to be tucked inside an Italian restaurant, but you can see some of the coolest kicks proudly displayed against an industrial red-brick wall at the popular Darkalino's restaurant. *11am-8pm Tue-Sat*

It's All Fun & Games

Magic Mouse Toys
57 B1

Brimming with puzzles, books, board games, stuffed animals and more, this is every kid's dream. Even cooler, it makes use of its historic underground section – yes, like the Underground tours (p63) – for even more inventory. *11am-6pm*

Tabletop Village
58 G5

This family-owned gaming shop is a hub for Pokémon enthusiasts, complete with Pokémon Trading Card Game (TCG) tournaments, trading days and more. *1-8pm Wed & Thu, 11am-8pm Fri & Sat, 11am-6pm Sun*

Pink Gorilla Games
59 E4

Rare retro games from the old-school Nintendo and Atari days, new releases, toys and collectables – you'll find it all at this neon-pink shop in the International District. *11am-7pm*

See p86
for eating,
drinking and
shopping
listings

Explore

Belltown & Seattle Center

Together, Belltown and Seattle Center function as one of the main hubs for Seattle visitors. Many opt to take in the landmark attractions of the latter – Chihuly Garden and Glass, MoPOP and the ever-iconic Space Needle, just to name a few – before venturing into neighboring Belltown each evening. There, trendy art galleries, delicious restaurants, craft cocktail bars and buzzy nightlife venues dominate the scene, making for an incredible, but still relatively chill, night on the town. It's also a popular spot to stay, with gems like the Edgewater Hotel and the Kimpton Palladian Hotel calling this neighborhood home.

Getting Around

 **Monorail**

The monorail ($4 one way) is the easiest way to get around Belltown and Seattle Center – after all, it was built with visitors in mind! It has just two stops: one just outside of Belltown neighborhood limits in Westlake Center, and the other in Seattle Center. You can also use your ORCA card on the monorail.

 **On Foot**

All in all, Belltown and Seattle Center are only about a mile across, so it's easy enough to walk where you want to go – but be prepared for some steep hills.

Space Needle (p76)
CDRIN/SHUTTERSTOCK

THE BEST

ICONIC LANDMARK
Space Needle (p76)

ARTSY ATTRACTION
Chihuly Garden & Glass (p78)

MEAL NEAR THE SPACE NEEDLE
Tilikum Place Cafe (p86)

EVENING PERFORMANCE
Pacific Northwest Ballet (p84)

DETROIT-STYLE PIZZA
Moto Pizza (p86)

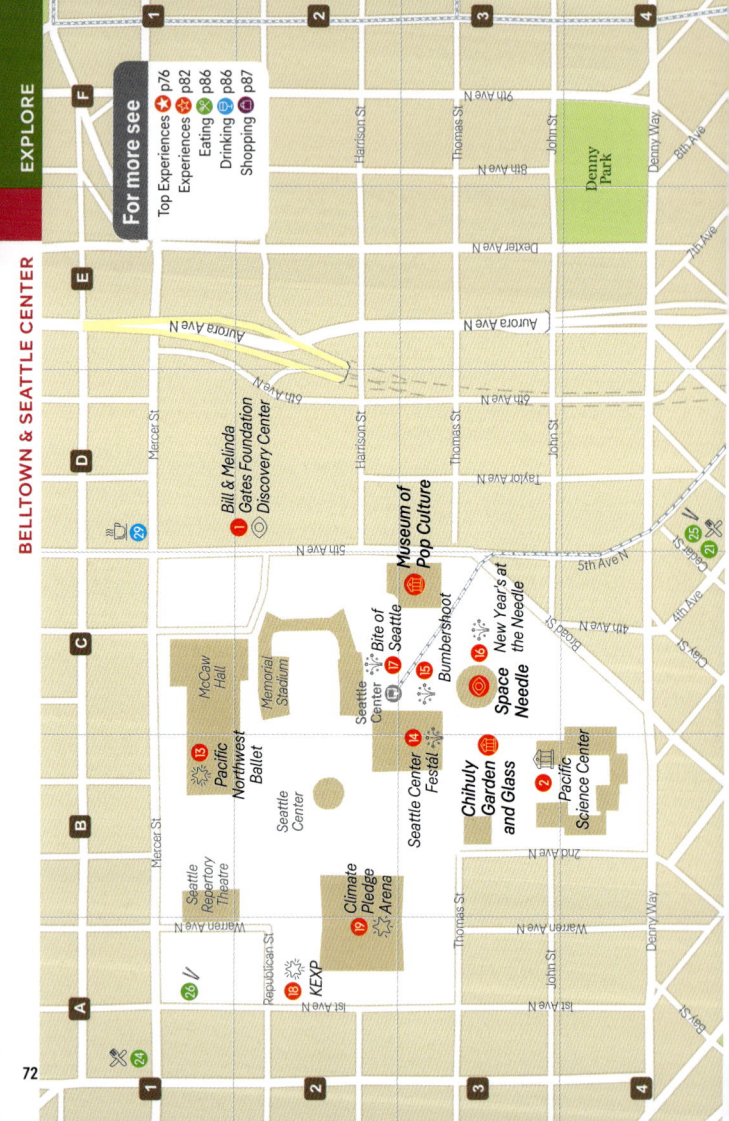

For more see

Top Experiences ✕ p76
Experiences ✕ p82
Eating ✕ p86
Drinking 🍺 p86
Shopping 🛍 p87

Denny Park

Bill & Melinda
Gates Foundation
① Discovery Center

Museum of
Pop Culture

Bite of
Seattle

Bumbershoot

New Year's at
the Needle

Space
Needle

McCaw
Hall

Memorial
Stadium

Pacific
Science Center

Seattle
Center

Northwest
Ballet

Pacific
Northwest
Ballet ⑬

Seattle Center
Festál ⑭

Chihuly
Garden
and Glass

Pacific
Science Center

② Pacific
Science Center

Seattle
Repertory
Theatre

Climate
Pledge
Arena ⑲

KEXP

⑱

8th Ave

7th Ave

5

33

4

38

54

Spheres

23

11

Dimitriou's Jazz Alley

Lenora St

Virginia St

5th Ave

6

4th Ave

7

8

Stewart St

F

Siff Cinema Downtown

12

Virginia St

2nd Ave

1st Ave

Pike Place Market

E

Bell St

28

3

Seattle Glassblowing Studio

Blanchard St

4th Ave

5th Ave

3rd Ave

Jupiter Bar

9

32

Pine St

35

Victor Steinbrueck Park

Battery St

Regrade Park

2nd Ave

36

1st Ave

30

Western Ave

Elliott Ave

D

Vue Lounge

Rendezvous

7

6

31

Wall St

4th Ave

39

Bell St

Battery St

57

3rd Ave

8

Vinnie's

10

Crocodile

2nd Ave

1st Ave

Cedar St

Clay St

Vine St

Wall St

Western Ave

Elliott Ave

Alaskan Way

C

27

B

Broad St

Western Ave

Elliott Ave

5

Olympic Sculpture Park

22

Elliott Ave W

Battery St

Bell St

Alaskan Way

20

FRS Clipper

Elliott Bay

A

N

400 m

0.2 miles

0

0

🚶 WALKING TOUR

The Beautiful Murals of Belltown

One of Seattle's artsiest districts, Belltown is home to loads of creatives at work. Recently, the City of Seattle funded the Hope Corps Downtown Mural Project, spanning five different neighborhoods, with many murals clustered in Belltown. Tour these art pieces during the Belltown Art Walk (every second Friday of the month), or head out on your own at any time.

START	END	LENGTH
Cosmic Heartbeat and *The Raid Murals*	*Ocean Dreams* Mural	1 mile; 45min

① Parking Lot Paintings

Start your mural meanderings at the parking lot on the intersection of 5th Ave and Bell St. There, you'll find two side-by-side art pieces: **Cosmic Heartbeat** by AO Hammer and **The Raid** by Stevie Shao. Together the pair make for a juxtaposed sight, with moody, deep colors in the former and bright, color-blocked sections in the latter.

② Surfing the Swells

From there, head southwest on Bell St until hitting Third Ave, where you'll find Revel Consulting, and, more import-antly, the incredible **Seaspray** mural. Painted as a collaboration between popular local artists Craig Cundiff and Sam Sneke, this art piece combines realistic waves with wildstyle graffiti lettering to create a one-of-a-kind piece of surf art.

③ An Artistic Hideaway

Seattle-based artist Joe Nix created what is now known as the **Belltown Corridor**, a hidden alleyway filled with some of the coolest murals in the city. To find the entrance, walk along Bell St between 2nd Ave and 3rd Ave. When you enter this backstreet, you'll be surrounded by murals in all styles – from modern urban realism to muted abstract works. Exit two blocks down at Lenora St.

④ A WNBA Legend

Sue Bird is widely regarded as one of the best WNBA players of all time, helping her team win Olympic gold medals and WNBA championships left and right. She played for the Seattle Storm through the entirety of her career, from 2002 to 2022. Today, a beautiful **Sue Bird Mural** – painted by local artist Craig Cundiff – is proudly displayed on the outer wall of Vann Studio Salon.

⑤ Seattle in Paint

Just a block west on First Ave lies another stunning mural: **Symbiotic** by Nalisha Estrellas. Sitting pretty on the outdoor wall of the Black Cat Bar, this art piece uses bright, bold colors to showcase the best of Seattle – from orcas to salmon to the always eye-catching Space Needle. Feel free to simply admire the painting or make use of it as an Instagram-worthy backdrop.

⑥ A Tribute to Orcas

The orca trend carries over to the final mural of the walk, **Ocean Dreams** by Adry del Rocio on Elliot Way. Painted in partnership with the UN Environment Programme (UNEP) and Street Art for Mankind (SAP), this colorful mural of sea life is meant to encourage viewers to think about and protect Seattle's – and the world's – marine ecosystems.

★ TOP EXPERIENCE

Space Needle

If there's one attraction that comes to mind when you think of Seattle, it's undoubtedly the Space Needle. Standing proudly at 605ft tall, this UFO-inspired tower was originally built for the 1962 World's Fair and continues to welcome about a million visitors each year.

MAP P72 **C3**

PLANNING TIP
The Space Needle uses dynamic pricing, so you'll get the best deals during the low season and on weekdays.

History of the Space Needle

Originally called the 'Space Cage', the **Space Needle** *(spaceneedle.com; adult/child from $35/30)* was designed by Victor Steinbrueck and John Graham Jr in the late 1950s and early 1960s, reportedly based on the napkin scribblings of World's Fair organizer Eddie Carlson. The iconic structure was modeled after a UFO – it was the Space Race era, after all, so everything celestial was all the rage. The Needle was constructed in less than a year and proved to be an instant hit; 2.3 million people paid $1 to ascend it during the World's Fair, which ran for six months between April and October 1962.

Sky-High Views

Take one of the sparkling new two-story glass elevators to the top of the Space Needle, where two viewing decks await. Find the outdoor observation deck on the upper level, taking in the views of Puget Sound, the city of Seattle, Mt Rainier and even Mt Saint Helens from 520ft up, all framed by tilted, clear-glass panels. If you'd prefer to stay inside, the floor-to-ceiling windows provide an exceptional viewing experience.

Scan for information on transportation, hours and more.

ULF NAMMERT/SHUTTERSTOCK

Just below the outdoor observation deck, you'll find the Loupe, or the revolving deck. It takes 30 minutes to do a full circumnavigation, and you can spot loads of Seattle attractions along the way.

Dining at 600ft High

Stick around on the top of the Space Needle a little longer with a bite to eat. For something quick and easy, try the flaky, buttery, vaguely Space Needle–shaped pies from TipTop Cafe (upper observation deck and ground floor): think everything from Yakima peach pies to beef and IPA pies.

For a more substantial meal, consider the Loupe Lounge (21+ only). Only open during the low season (fall to spring), this rotating restaurant serves up four-course PNW-inspired food towers to go along with the epic city views.

TAKE A BREAK
Escape from the crowds with a drink at one of the two sectioned-off bars: the **Sunset Bar** (on the upper level) and the **Revolving Bar** (on the lower Loupe level).

⭐ **TOP EXPERIENCE**

Chihuly Garden & Glass

This exquisite exposition of the life and work of dynamic local sculptor Dale Chihuly is possibly the finest collection of curated glass art you'll ever see. It shows off Chihuly's creative designs in a suite of interconnected rooms and an adjacent garden in the shadow of the Space Needle.

MAP P72 **B3**

PLANNING TIP
Buy a combo ticket that includes both the Space Needle and Chihuly Garden and Glass for a discount on both attractions. You will need to visit both attractions on one day.

Scan to pair your visit with the free audio tour.

The Exhibition Rooms

Begin with a stroll through eight **exhibition rooms** *(chihulygardenandglass.com; adult/child from $32/ free)*, each offering another of Dale Chihuly's takes on glass. The first standout sculpture is Sealife Tower within the larger Sealife Room, a huge azure structure of intricately blown glass that looks as if it has sprung straight out of Poseidon's lair. Look out for the small octopuses and starfish melded into the swirling waves. Then, there's the Persian Ceiling. Technically empty apart from one single wooden bench, this exhibition room is awash with color, from the kaleidoscopic puzzle of layered glass pieces laid atop a glass ceiling.

Soon after, you'll find the Ikebana & Float Boat, consisting of a pair of boats overflowing with round glass balls. The display was inspired by Chihuly's time in Venice, where he casually threw luminous glass spheres into the canals and watched as local children enthusiastically collected them in boats.

Towards the end lies the Macchia Forest, a rather unassuming set of oversized bowls. The secrets lie within the glass – take your phone flashlight and shine it onto the bowls. It'll reveal a whole new set of colors, ones tucked away into the eight layers of multicolored glass.

CHRISTIAN HEINZ/SHUTTERSTOCK

The Glasshouse

Sitting like a giant greenhouse under the Space Needle, the Glasshouse offers a nod to London's erstwhile Crystal Palace, one of Chihuly's most important historical inspirations. You'll notice that the floor space of the Glasshouse has been left empty, drawing your eye up to the ceiling where a huge medley of flower-shaped glass pieces imitate the reds, oranges and yellows of a perfect sunset.

The Garden

Chihuly uses the garden to demonstrate the seamless melding of glass art and natural vegetation. Many of the alfresco pieces are simple pointed shards of glass redolent of luminescent reeds, but the real eye-catcher is The Sun, a riot of twisted yellow 'flames' whose swirling brilliance erases the heaviness of the most overcast Seattle sky.

TAKE A BREAK
Along the perimeter of the Glasshouse, you'll find several benches, great for giving your legs a rest and admiring the art.

⭐ **TOP EXPERIENCE**

Museum of Pop Culture

The Museum of Pop Culture – or MoPOP – is an inspired marriage between super-modern architecture and legendary rock-and-roll history. Inside its avant-garde frame, you can tune into the famous sounds of Seattle or attempt to imitate the rock masters in an Interactive 'Sound Lab'.

MAP P72 **C3**

PLANNING TIP
Planning on visiting a bunch of major Seattle attractions in addition to MoPOP? Save some money with CityPass, which offers three- or five-attraction bundles.

Scan for information on accessibility, hours and more.

Eye-Catching Architecture

Before you even step inside of **MoPOP** (*mopop. org; adult/child from $25/19*), its architecture will undoubtedly catch your eye. With its crinkled folds and smooth curves colored in metallic blues and purples, this highly unusual building was designed by renowned Canadian architect Frank Gehry, a strong proponent of deconstructivism. Gehry – who designed the equally outlandish Guggenheim Museum in Bilbao, Spain, and the Walt Disney Concert Hall in Los Angeles, California – supposedly used one of Hendrix's smashed-up guitars as his inspiration.

Making Music

The main exhibit hall is anchored by If VI Was IX, a tower of 700 instruments designed by German-born artist Trimpin. Many of the permanent exhibits center on Hendrix, including the Fender Stratocaster guitar that he played at Woodstock in 1969. There's also a nostalgic slice of grunge memorabilia in a section entitled 'Nirvana: Taking Punk to the Masses'. Framing it all, you'll find an exhibit called Massive: The Power of Pop Culture, which highlights the many ways that pop culture can be used to enact change and build communities.

ACHINTHAMB/SHUTTERSTOCK

But MoPOP isn't your typical museum. It's not just about admiring musical icons of history; it's about fostering your own musical talent. Most of the 3rd floor of MoPOP is given over to the interactive Sound Lab, where you can lay down vocal tracks, play instruments, fiddle with effects pedals and – best of all – jam in several mini studios.

Movie Magic

Despite its love for rock-and-roll, MoPOP covers more than just music. After all, that's just one facet of pop culture. On Level 2, the entire South Galleries wing is dedicated to the different genres in the film industry. Peruse loads of Star Wars film props and memorabilia in the Sci-Fi section, get spooked by Michael's mask in the Horror section, or peek at the Cowardly Lion costume from *The Wizard of Oz* in the Fantasy section, just to start.

TAKE A BREAK
The **Artists at Play** playground and park is just outside MoPOP, complete with benches and picnic tables, perfect for a break or snack.

EXPERIENCES

Feel Inspired at the Bill & Melinda Gates Foundation Discovery Center
MUSEUM

MAP: **1** P72 **D2**

The work of the Bill & Melinda Gates Foundation is celebrated at this suitably high-tech visitor center, part of a larger foundation building located opposite the Space Needle. Spread over a few rooms with highly interactive exhibits, this **center** (*discovergates.org; free*) lays out the Gates' bios and shows examples of their ongoing humanitarian and research work around the world, including ending polio in India and fighting malaria across the African continent.

Get Hands on at the Pacific Science Center
MUSEUM

MAP: **2** P72 **B3**

In the heart of Seattle Center among the big-name attractions like the Space Needle and MoPOP lies the **Pacific Science Center** (*pacificsciencecenter.org; adult/child from $26/20*). This hands-on museum is the perfect place to reignite a love for science, for both kids and adults alike. Say hello to some fluttering friends at the Tropical Butterfly House, learn about celestial exploration through the immersive Planetarium experience, or travel back to prehistoric times through the Dinosaurs: A Journey Through Time exhibit. For an extra cost, you can also enjoy the immersive music-and-light-filled experiences

of the Laser Dome and catch the latest movies in the high-quality IMAX theater.

Try Your Hand at Glass Art at a Seattle Glass-blowing Studio Class
ART CLASS

MAP: **3** P72 **E5**

After taking in the glass pieces at Chihuly Garden and Glass (p78), you might be inspired to try your own hand at glass blowing – that's where **Seattle Glassblowing Studio** (*seattleglassblowing.com*) comes into play. This renowned hot shop offers beginner-friendly glass-blowing classes (starting at $85/piece), where you can make cups, bowls, ornaments or vases.

Take a Tour of the Jungle-esque Amazon Spheres
ARCHITECTURE

MAP: **4** P72 **F5**

Amazon – as in, the Seattle-started online retailer – pretty much dominates a small neighborhood just east of Belltown known as the Denny Triangle. On this Amazon campus, you'll find a couple of Amazon Go stores, a pair of Community Banana Stands (grab a free banana when you pass!) and several Amazon corporate buildings – the latter of which includes the eye-catching **Spheres** (*seattlespheres.com*).

From the outside, these three geometric glass spheres are already an architectural marvel. But if you look closer, you might realize that these spheres are filled with plants – 40,000 of them, to be a little more exact. While certain Amazon corporate employees have easy access to this greenhouse-esque space, it's much harder for the average Joe to get in. It's only open to the public on the first and third Saturdays of each month, with a limited number of reservation slots released 15 days in advance. Once you're in though, you'll be in awe of the botanical biosphere that's tucked inside.

Stroll the Waterfront at the Olympic Sculpture Park

SCULPTURE PARK

MAP: **5** P72 **A5**

This **sculpture park** *(seattle artmuseum.org/visit/olympic-sculpture-park)*, which is an ingenuous feat of urban planning, is an official offshoot of the Seattle Art Museum (p50) and bears the same strong eye toward design and curation. There are more than 20 sculptures to stop at and admire in this green space that sprawls out over reclaimed urban decay. You can also enjoy them in passing while traversing the park's winding trails. Views of Puget Sound and the Olympic Peninsula in the background will delight anyone looking to snap some great pictures.

Oh, the Entertainment Options You'll Find

NIGHTLIFE

Belltown is packed with evening entertainment options, with 2nd Ave being the epicenter. **Rendezvous** (MAP: **6** P72 **D6**; *the rendezvous.rocks*) has a wide array of events – from dance parties to comedy shows to live theater productions. Next door at **Vue Lounge** (MAP: **7** P72 **D6**; *vueseattle. com*), dance the night away to hip-hop and EDM beats. Of course, there's a slew of bars, including the classy **Vinnie's** (MAP: **8** P72 **C6**; *vinniesseattle.com*) and the arcade-game-filled **Jupiter Bar** (MAP: **9** P72 **E7**; *jupiterbarseattle.com*).

Not far off this entertainment thoroughfare, you'll also find the **Crocodile** (MAP: **10** P72 **C6**; *the crocodile.com*), a grunge music icon, and **Dimitriou's Jazz Alley** (MAP: **11** P72 **F6**; *jazzalley.com/www-home*), a legacied jazz venue.

Alternatively, catch an indie movie at the **SIFF Cinema Downtown** (MAP: **12** P72 **F6**; *siff.net/cinema/cinema-venues/siff-cinema-downtown); adult/child $20/15)*, a bag of locally beloved chocolate popcorn in hand.

 IT HAPPENED AT THE WORLD'S FAIR

Known officially as the Century 21 Exposition, Seattle's 1962 World's Fair set out to depict the future, as envisaged through the eyes of an affluent Cold War generation – hence the UFO-shaped Space Needle as the newly built centerpiece. The fair attracted 10 million visitors, garnered many plaudits and turned a tidy profit. It also helped cement Seattle as a top-tier American city.

SEATTLE: THE BIRTHPLACE OF GRUNGE

Grunge emerged in Seattle in the 1980s as a reaction against the perceived excesses of 1980s hair metal and mainstream rock. Bands like Green River, Mudhoney and The Melvins blended the raw energy of punk rock with the heavy, distorted sounds of metal, often played at a slower tempo, creating the gritty, sludgy sound that grunge is known for. Initially many artists disliked the 'grunge' label, (accurately) viewing it as a marketing term. However, as the genre gained mainstream popularity in the early 1990s, with bands like Nirvana, Pearl Jam, Soundgarden and Alice in Chains, the term became widely accepted, even if begrudgingly by some, as a descriptor for this unique 'Seattle Sound'.

Or watch a stunning performance by the **Pacific Northwest Ballet** (MAP: **13** P72 **B1**; *pnb.org*), a leading American ballet company that is incredibly forward-thinking regarding who can be a ballet dancer, with talented BIPOC, nonbinary, and transgender dancers flourishing in the troupe.

Learn About Different Cultures Through Seattle Center Festál   EVENT

MAP: **14** P72 **B3**

Seattle Center Festál (*seattle center.com/events/featured-events/festal*)is a series of 25 annual festivals celebrating cultures and the diversity of the greater Seattle community, all of which showcase identities across the globe through food, music, dance, visual arts and so much more.

Experience the Best of the Arts at Bumbershoot   EVENT

MAP: **15** P72 **C3**

Bumbershoot (*bumbershoot.com; from $150*) is an internationally renowned arts and music festival that takes place at the Seattle Center every Labor Day weekend. This multidisciplinary extravaganza showcases everything from music and dance to comedy and visual arts.

Over the years, legendary musicians like Kendrick Lamar, Tina Turner and The Beastie Boys have graced its stages. Comedy giants like Jerry Seinfeld and Whoopi Goldberg have brought the laughs, too. Alongside these international stars, this locally sponsored event works to bring local Seattle artists of all kinds into the spotlight as well.

Spend New Years at the Needle   EVENT

MAP: **16** P72 **C3**

Seattle isn't often thought of as a New Year's destination, and that's a shame, because the city – and the **Space Needle** (*space needle.com/newyears*) in particular – goes all out. With drones and pyrotechnics, this event will create a New Year's celebration to remember.

84

Eat Your Way Through Bite of Seattle

EVENT

MAP: ⑰ P72 **C2**

Sample delicious food and drinks from local Seattle restaurants and vendors at this massively popular July **food festival** *(biteofseattle.com)*. Complete with cooking demonstrations, eating competitions and live-music performances, it makes for an unforgettable weekend.

Experience Everything KEXP Has to Offer

MUSIC VENUE

MAP: ⑱ P72 **A1**

KEXP *(kexp.org)* is primarily a non-commercial radio station that focuses on indie music. You can listen to its tunes online or via your streaming platform of choice as you explore all around the neighborhood.

Even cooler, you can visit in person. Watch the radio hosts at work through their live in-studio public viewing sessions, or listen to live music at its cozy music venue, the Gathering Space at KEXP. Even if the timing doesn't line up to see a live performance, a visit to its Light in the Attic Record Shop and Vita @ KEXP coffee shop are treats for music lovers and coffee fans, respectively.

Catch a Seattle Kraken Game

SPORTS

MAP: ⑲ P72 **A2**

The **Climate Pledge Arena** *(climatepledgearena.com)* is an incredibly cool venue, in more ways than one. Firstly, it officially became zero-carbon-certified in October 2023. It's powered by 100% renewable energy, implements on-site waste sorting to prioritize zero-waste initiatives, and uses captured rainwater to make the Kraken's ice hockey rink, just to start.

While these sustainable features are incredible in their own right, the Seattle Kraken brings even more excitement. Officially joining the NHL in 2021, this pro-hockey team has already made its mark, qualifying for the Stanley Cup playoffs in 2023 and amassing thousands of die-hard fans in just a few years. The atmosphere at a Kraken game is electric, so don your team jersey and join in on the fun.

The legendary WNBA team **Seattle Storm** *(storm.wnba.com)*, also calls the Climate Pledge Arena home. Owned by a team of Seattle businesswomen, the team has garnered 16 playoff appearances and four championships under its belt since its establishment in 2000.

Go Whale-Watching Aboard the FRS Clipper

BOAT TOUR

MAP: ⑳ P72 **A7**

Many species of whales like to call Puget Sound their home. Orcas hang out year-round, while other species visit between March and October. Hop aboard the **FRS Clipper** *(clippervacations.com/ seattle-day-trips/seattle-whale-watching-tour; adult/child from $104/52)* for a glimpse of these majestic marine mammals in their natural habitat.

See p72 for map of locations

Best Places for...

💲 Budget 💲💲 Midrange 💲💲💲 Top End

Eating

In-Demand European-Inspired Restaurants

Tilikum Place Cafe 💲💲

 D4

Near the Space Needle, this seasonal, European-style cafe is beloved by locals for lunch, brunch, dinner and dessert. Make reservations. *10am-2pm Thu & Fri, 9am-2pm Sat & Sun, plus 5-9pm Thu-Sat*

Moto Pizza 💲💲

22 **A5**

With multi-month-long wait times, you have to plan in advance to get the topping-ladden, Detroit-style goodness that is a pie from Moto Pizza. You can't go wrong with the popular Mr Pig, featuring *lechon* (pork belly) and *calamansi* lime sauce. *11am-9pm*

Willmott's Ghost 💲💲

 F6

Led by James Beard Award–winning chef Renee Erickson, Wilmott's Ghost is known for its Roman-style pizzas and focaccias. Even better, it is located within the hard-to-access Amazon Spheres. *11:30am-9pm Mon-Fri, 4-9pm Sat*

Flavorful Mexican Eats

Sal Y Limon 💲💲

 A1

This bright and lively cantina is known for its handmade tortillas and next-level margaritas. *11am-9pm Sun-Thu, to 11pm Fri & Sat*

Impeccable Asian Food

Wa'Z 💲💲💲

25 **D4**

Fresh ingredients and artful, flavorful cooking are the highlights of the *kaiseki* (multi-course Japanese tasting menu) at Wa'Z. Grab a seat at the bar. *6-8pm Wed & Thu, 5-10pm Fri & Sat, 1-7pm Sun*

CÔBA 💲

26 **A1**

All of the noodle soups – especially the oxtail and short rib pho – are a treat. There are also gluten-free bread options

with a dedicated fryer. *11am-10pm Sun-Thu, to midnight Fri & Sat*

PNW Flavors & Waterfront Views

Six Seven Restaurant 💲💲💲

27 **B7**

Hidden in the Edgewater Hotel, Six Seven Restaurant offers a refined dining experience with high-quality Pacific Northwest ingredients. Time your meal with sunset to see the Cascade Mountains and Puget Sound in a gorgeous golden glow. *hours vary*

Drinking

An Expertly Made Espresso

Fulcrum Cafe

28 **E5**

This Belltown cafe is known for its single-origin coffee and its incredible fun latte flavors. Cream of pistachio latte, anyone? *7am-6pm Mon-Fri, 8am-6pm Sat & Sun*

Konvene Coffee

 D1

Just outside Seattle Center, this sleek coffee shop has incredible breakfast sandwiches to go with your coffee of choice. *9am-3:30pm Mon-Fri, to 2pm Sat*

Good Times on Tap

Cloudburst Brewing

 D8

Cloudburst Brewing features hoppy beers with sassy names. The bare-bones tasting room is always packed. *4-9pm Wed, 2-9pm Thu, 2-10pm Fri, noon-10pm Sat, noon-8pm Sun*

Just the Tap

31 **D7**

An all-around feel-good spot. It's pizza by the slice, 24 self-serve pour taps with well-curated beers and ciders, pinball machines, board games and trivia nights. *11am-11pm Sun-Thu, to 1am Fri & Sat*

Cocktail Creations

Whisky Bar

32 **E7**

Try a whiskey flight to find your favorite variation, or choose an innovative cocktail from the relatively short, but clearly mastered menu. *2pm-2am Mon-Thu, noon-2am Fri-Sun*

Deep Dive

see **F5**

Reserve early to get a seat at this classy, vintage-inspired bar inside of the Amazon Spheres. *4-10pm Sun-Wed, to 11pm Thu-Sat*

Phocific Standard Time

33 **F6**

Chase a pho-fat-washed shot of Jameson with incredibly flavorful broth at this speakeasy. *5-11pm Tue-Thu, to midnight Fri & Sat*

Zesty & Zingy

Rachel's Ginger Beer

34 **F5**

A Seattle institution with zingy ginger-based drinks that pack a punch – in its original non-alcoholic form or mixed into a fun cocktail. *11:30am-8pm Mon-Sat*

Shopping

Music & Art

Steinbrueck Native Gallery

35 **E8**

Bringing Indigenous artists into the spotlight, this gallery showcases Northwest Coast, Arctic and Alaskan art. *11am-5pm*

Singles Going Steady

36 **D7**

Singles Going Steady – named after an album by British punk pioneers the Buzzcocks – is a niche record store specializing in punk, oi, reggae and ska, mostly in the form of 7in vinyl singles. *noon-6pm Tue-Sat*

Botanical Retail

Bakeree

37 **C5**

The 'budtenders' at this marijuana dispensary are informed and happy to help you find the right product for you – whether its flowers, edibles, topicals or something else. *8am-11:45pm*

Bouquet

38 **F5**

This absolutely adorable flower shop sells beautiful bouquets – both premade and custom made – as well as all sorts of plant-related accessories. *10am-5:30pm Mon-Fri, to 5pm Sat*

Gourmet Food Goods

Mixed Pantry

39 **D7**

Sauces are the name of the game at this curated gourmet food store. If you really want to get into it, book a soy-sauce or chili-crisp flight tasting. *11am-7pm Wed-Sat, to 4pm Sun*

87

See p96
for eating,
drinking and
shopping
listings

Explore
Queen Anne & Magnolia

Though the popular Seattle Center area is technically part of Queen Anne, the rest of this hilltop neighborhood – and next door Magnolia – have a completely different atmosphere than the bustling Space Needle hub. Here, you'll instead find elaborate homes and mansions perched on hilly streets, quiet parks with blooming flowers, and some of the best views of the Seattle skyline. Bracketing these two neighborhoods, you'll find Discovery Park and its endlessly green trails to the east, and the beautiful Lake Union – and all of the water activities that come with it – to the west.

Getting Around

Bus

Queen Anne and Magnolia may be the neighborhoods with the most limited public transportation options in Seattle, with only buses servicing the area.

 Rideshare

Between the limited public transportation, the steep hills and the sometimes hard-to-find parking, rideshares aren't a bad option when navigating around Queen Anne and Magnolia.

Car

A car isn't a bad option in these areas either. The major sites typically have a decent amount of street parking (or even designated lots!), though parking will likely be a struggle at certain restaurants and shops.

Kenmore Air (p94), Lake Union
OKSANA.PERKINS/SHUTTERSTOCK

THE BEST

WATERFRONT HIKE
Cheshiahud Loop (p95)

SEATTLE SKYLINE VIEWS
Kerry Park (p93)

SEAPLANE OUTFITTER
Kenmore Air (p94)

COZY COFFEE SHOP
Caffè Fiore (p97)

SWEET TREAT
Nutty Squirrel Gelato (p96)

EXPLORE

QUEEN ANNE & MAGNOLIA

A **B** **C** **D**

1

Discovery Park

Discovery Park Blvd ❶

Salmon Bay

Ballard Bridge

W Government Way

W Commodore Way

W Emerson St

🍺 23

🏛 13

W Emerson Pl

Lawton Park

W Manor Pl

W Ruffner St

2

W Bertona St

W Bertona St

W Dravus St

W Dravus St

W Dravus St

W Armour St

3

MAGNOLIA

Interbay Athletic Field

🧁 16

W Mc Graw St

W Mc Graw St

W Boston St

INTERBAY

W Newton St

W Wheeler St

4

🔭 ❷

Magnolia Viewpoint

Southwest Queen Anne Greenbelt

Magnolia Blvd W

Magnolia Blvd W

Magnolia Blvd W

🍺 22

W Galer St

W Galer St

Elliott Ave W

5

❹ ❄

Kenmore Air

Museum of History & Industry 🏛

Lake Union

❻

🏛 ❸

Center for Wooden Boats

Lake Union Park

❼

Cheshiahud Loop

🚶 ❽

Elliott Bay

6

Broad St

Valley St

Valley St

Lake Union Park

Valley St

0 _____ 200 m
0 _____ 0.1 miles

A **B** **C** **D**

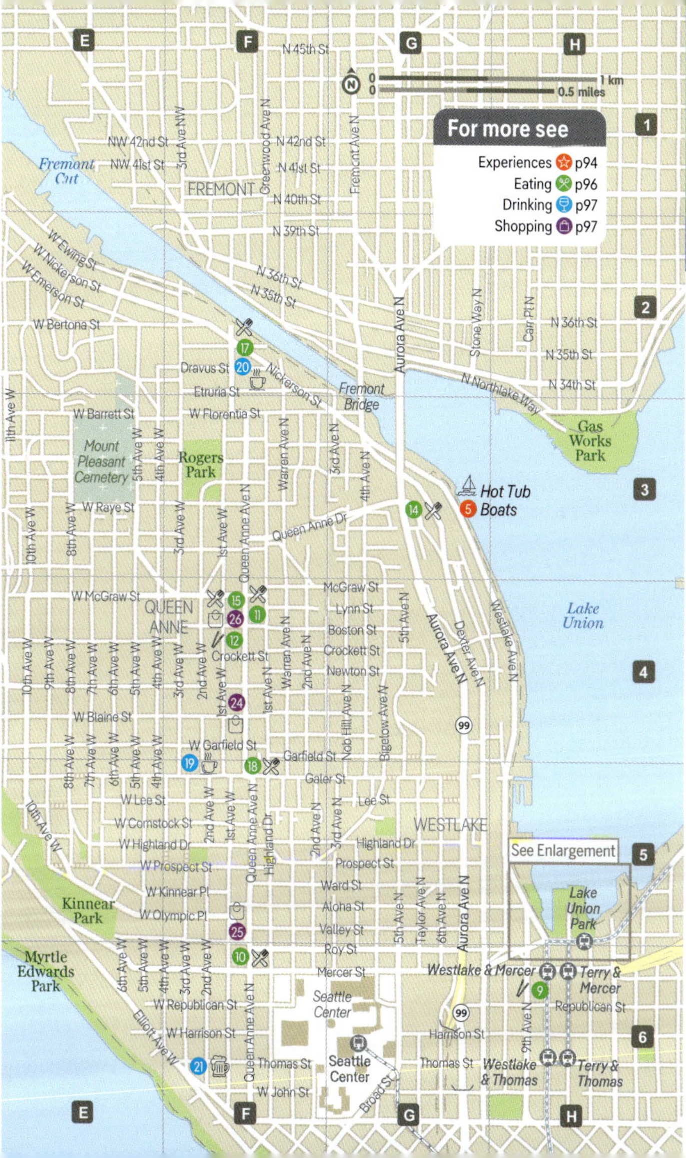

Map Labels

Grid references (top): E, F, G, H

Grid references (right side): 1, 2, 3, 4, 5, 6

For more see
Experiences p94
Eating p96
Drinking p97
Shopping p97

0 — 1 km
0 — 0.5 miles

N 45th St
N 42nd St
NW 42nd St
NW 41st St
N 41st St
Greenwood Ave N
Fremont Ave N
Fremont Cut
FREMONT
N 40th St
N 39th St
3rd Ave NW
N 36th St
N 35th St
W Ewing St
W Nickerson St
W Emerson St
W Bertona St
Aurora Ave N
Stone Way N
Carr Pl N
N 36th St
N 35th St
N 34th St
N Northlake Way
Dravus St
Etruria St
W Florentia St
Nickerson St
Fremont Bridge
Fremont Bridge
Gas Works Park
W Barrett St
11th Ave W
5th Ave W
4th Ave W
Mount Pleasant Cemetery
Rogers Park
3rd Ave W
1st Ave W
Queen Anne Ave N
Warren Ave N
3rd Ave N
4th Ave N
Aurora Ave N
Dexter Ave N
Westlake Ave N
W Raye St
Queen Anne Dr
Hot Tub Boats
Lake Union
W McGraw St
QUEEN ANNE
McGraw St
Lynn St
Boston St
Crockett St
Newton St
Crockett St
W Blaine St
10th Ave W
9th Ave W
8th Ave W
7th Ave W
6th Ave W
5th Ave W
4th Ave W
3rd Ave W
2nd Ave W
1st Ave W
Warren Ave N
1st Ave N
2nd Ave N
Nob Hill Ave N
Bigelow Ave N
Aurora Ave N
99
W Garfield St
Garfield St
Galer St
Lee St
W Lee St
W Comstock St
W Highland Dr
W Prospect St
WESTLAKE
Highland Dr
3rd Ave N
Prospect St
Ward St
Aloha St
Valley St
Roy St
5th Ave N
Taylor Ave N
6th Ave N
See Enlargement
Lake Union Park
W Kinnear Pl
W Olympic Pl
Kinnear Park
Highland Dr
10th Ave W
6th Ave W
5th Ave W
4th Ave W
3rd Ave W
Queen Anne Ave N
Mercer St
Seattle Center
Westlake & Mercer
Terry & Mercer
9th Ave N
Republican St
Myrtle Edwards Park
Elliott Ave W
W Republican St
W Harrison St
W John St
Thomas St
Seattle Center
Broad St
Harrison St
99
Thomas St
Westlake & Thomas
Terry & Thomas
Westlake & Thomas

17, 20, 14, 5, 15, 11, 26, 12, 24, 19, 18, 25, 10, 21, 9

WALKING TOUR

Scenic Spots in Queen Anne

Much of Queen Anne is settled atop the 456ft Queen Anne Hill. With this higher elevation comes incredible views of Downtown Seattle, Puget Sound, Mt Rainier and the Olympic Mountains on clear days. As you stroll from one lookout point to another, take in the high-end homes and their fin-de-siècle architecture all along the way.

START	END	LENGTH
Bhy Kracke Park	West Queen Anne Retaining Walls	1.2 miles; 45min

❶ A Hidden Viewpoint

Usually only visited by the residents that live nearby, **Bhy Kracke Park** (*seattle.gov/parks/allparks/bhy-kracke-park*) is a bit of a hidden gem. Beyond the playground, picnic tables and short walking trails, this park offers incredible views of the Seattle skyline – including the iconic Space Needle, of course. You'll find the best lookout spot at the top of the park, which does require a bit of stair-climbing.

❷ A Scenic Stairway

There are stairways going up and down all of hilly Queen Anne, many of which offer incredible views of the city. One of the best is found at the intersection of **Ward St and Warren Ave N**. From the top of the stairway on a clear day, you'll be able to see the Space Needle, Puget Sound and even Mt Rainier in all their sparkling glory.

❸ Views & Company

Kerry Park (*seattle.gov/parks/allparks/kerry-park*) is the most well known of the Queen Anne viewpoints – and for good reason. Amid the glittering Beverly Hills–like homes of Highland Dr, everyone can enjoy eagle's-eye views of Downtown Seattle and Elliott Bay (and Mt Rainier, should it take its cloudy hat off) from this spectacular lookout.

❹ A Flowery Find

Parsons Gardens (*seattle.gov/parks/allparks/parsons-gardens*) feels like an undiscovered wonder when you stumble across it, especially after the crowds that can gather at Kerry Park. But the five-minute walk west through the expensive, well-cared-for homes leaves the pack behind. Though still offering stunning views of Puget Sound, Parsons Gardens' springtime flowers tend to steal the show, with pink magnolias, purple rhododendrons and blue hydrangeas, bright and blooming.

❺ A Trio of Benches

Just across the intersection from Parsons Gardens lies **Marshall Park** (*seattle.gov/parks/allparks/marshall-park*). Nothing more than a set of three benches and a tiny green space, this Queen Anne park offers a quiet atmosphere to go along with its gorgeous vistas. Clear days offer views of the Olympic Mountains on the other side of Puget Sound, and clear evenings bring postcard-worthy sunsets to go along with them.

❻ Pieces of History

Finish off your scenic stroll at the **West Queen Anne Retaining Walls**. Also called the Wilcox Walls, this landmark looks like it was pulled out of a European fairy tale, with its pointed archways and elaborate brick-tiled walls.

EXPERIENCES

Explore the Best of Discovery Park

PARK

MAP: **1** P90 **A1**

The main walking trail of **Discovery Park** (seattle.gov/x63689) is the 3-mile-long Loop Trail, part of a 12-mile trail network. Branch off onto the South Beach trail, descending down a steep bluff to view the still-functioning West Point Lighthouse, a great spot for panoramic views of the Sound and Olympic Mountains.

The park is also home to a couple of cultural and historic sites. The Daybreak Star Indian Cultural Center serves as the community center for the United Indians of All Tribes Foundation (UIATF) and showcases Native American art, culture and traditions.

On the other side of this massive green space lies Fort Lawton, an 1897 army base used during WWII.

Take in the Sights from Magnolia Viewpoint

PARK

MAP: **2** P90 **A4**

While there are lots of fantastic viewpoints in Queen Anne, hilly Magnolia has its fair share of scenic spots too, including the simply named **Magnolia Viewpoint**. It's a great location for a lovely picnic or sunset stroll, with Space Needle, Downtown Seattle and Puget Sound views the whole way through.

Sail Away with the Center for Wooden Boats

BOAT TOUR

MAP: **3** P90 **B6**

Honoring Seattle's historical, aquatic and Native American antecedents, this one-of-a-kind **museum and enthusiasts' center** (cwb.org) features vintage and replica boats and offers rentals. Best of all, however, are its free Sunday public sailboat rides on Lake Union (first come, first served; sign-ups start 10am).

Ride on a Seaplane with Kenmore Air

PLANE TOUR

MAP: **4** P90 **A5**

Take to the skies on a seaplane with **Kenmore Air** (kenmoreair.com/seattle-lake-union). With its 25-minute Seattle Scenic Seaplane Tour ($119), you'll head off the banks of Lake Union, first gliding across the surface of the lake, then soaring over the University of Washington, Elliott Bay and the Seattle city center.

Enjoy Lake Union from a Hot Tub Boat

BOAT TOUR

MAP: **5** P90 **G3**

There are a few ways to enjoy the beauty of Lake Union – on a scenic walk, from the air or from a kayak, just to name a few – but what about from a hot tub boat? The aptly named **Hot Tub Boats** (lakeunionhottubboats.com; from $400) is a wooden boat that is 80% hot tub. All you have to do is sit in the bubbling water and sail away.

WHERE DID QUEEN ANNE GET ITS NAME?

While most people tend to assume that Seattle's Queen Anne neighborhood was named after the relatively unknown 18th-century British monarch, that's not actually the case. Queen Anne was named after the style of architecture of the same name, which popped up quite a bit as the neighborhood was being built. This style is known for its asymmetrical facades, elaborate ornamentation and even turrets, and you can still see quite a few Queen Anne architectural buildings today.

Explore the Museum of History & Industry
MUSEUM

MAP: **6** P90 **B5**

Almost everything you need to know about Seattle is crammed into the fabulous **Museum of History & Industry** (*mohai.org; adult/child $25/free*), located on the southern shore of Lake Union. With an archive of over four million objects, MOHAI displays its stash of historical booty in an impressively repurposed naval armory building.

The big eye-catcher as you walk into the huge hangar-sized space is a 1919 Boeing airplane hanging from the roof (the first commercial Boeing ever made). Beyond that, there are countless interactive features across the exhibits – from building structurally sound bridges to controlling an ancient ship's steering wheel.

Enjoy the Views from Lake Union Park
PARK

MAP: **7** P90 **B6**

Opened in 2010, **Lake Union Park** (*seattle.gov/parks/allparks/lake-union-park*) occupies ex-navy land on the southern tip of Lake Union and has a wading pond (with model sailboats you can use), an attractive bridge and a boat launch.

It hosts the Museum of History & Industry in the old naval armory building and the Center for Wooden Boats. It's a lovely spot for watching the seaplanes, heading out on a kayaking adventure or simply soaking up the Seattle summer sunshine.

Circumnavigate Lake Union via the Cheshiahud Loop
HIKE

MAP: **8** P90 **A6**

Inaugurated years ago to tie in with the landscaping of Lake Union Park, this well-signposted **6-mile route** (*seattle.gov/parks/allparks/cheshiahud-lake-union-loop*) circumnavigates Lake Union by gelling together existing trails, sidewalks and paths.

Named for a Duwamish chief who once headed a lakeside village, it's a good way to keep away from busy roads while walking/jogging/cycling through at least five Seattle neighborhoods.

Best Places for...

$** Budget **$$** Midrange **$$$ Top End

See p90 for map of locations

Eating

Moderate Price, Bold Flavors

Paju $$

9 H6

A small and simple space that serves modern takes on beloved Korean dishes. *hours vary*

Toulouse Petit $$

10 F6

A Cajun-Creole restaurant with food, decor and ambience inspired by New Orleans. Don't miss the perfectly puffy buttermilk beignets. *10am-11pm Mon-Wed, 10am-midnight Thu & Fri, 9am-midnight Sat, 9am-11pm Sun*

How to Cook a Wolf $$

11 F4

This Ethan Stowell–run restaurant is all about making the most of limited ingredients, though you'd never guess based on the quality of the high-class, Mediterranean-inspired dishes. *4-10pm Sun-Thu, 4-11pm Fri & Sat, plus 10am-2pm Sat & Sun*

Isarn Thai Soul Kitchen $$

12 F4

Southern and Central Bangkok flavors are brought to life at this bustling restaurant in the heart of Queen Anne. Stop by during happy hour (3pm to 6pm daily) for the best appetizer and drink deals. *11am-9pm*

Fantastic Fish & Chips

Little Chinook's $

13 D1

What better place to get fresh seafood than at the Fisherman's Terminal, home to Little Chinook's? This casual takeout eatery is known for its fish and chips, with both crisp panko-breaded and lighter tempura options. *11:30am-6pm*

Award-Worthy Eateries

Canlis $$$

14 G3

One of Seattle's most celebrated restaurants, Canlis is old-school posh – it even has a dress code. Settle in for a traditional PNW meal and stunning views of Lake Union through the angled floor-to-ceiling windows. *5-11pm Tue, Wed Fri & Sat, to midnight Thu*

Eden Hill Restaurant $$$

15 F4

It's difficult to grab a table in this 24-seat restaurant, but if you're lucky enough to snag one, the innovative, seasonal dishes are sure to blow your taste buds away. *5-9pm Thu-Mon*

Sweet Treats

Nutty Squirrel Gelato $

16 B4

This award-winning, family-owned shop crafts small batches of high-quality gelato in fun flavors – like rose-petal panna cotta – and classic ones – like mint chip and espresso. *noon-9pm*

Byen Bakery $

17 F2

Buttery pastries await at the Danish-inspired Byen Bakery. The lingonberry danishes, *skolebrød* (custard-filled cardamom bun) and princes cakes in particular keep the crowds coming back again and again. *6am-5pm Mon-Fri, 6:30am-5pm Sat, 7am-4pm Sun*

Breakfast & Brunch

5 Spot 💲💲
18 **F5**

This cozy breakfast diner serves all the homey morning-meal classics – chicken 'n' waffles, huevos rancheros, French toast – you name it. *8am-9pm Mon-Wed, 7am-9pm Thu-Sat, 7am-4pm Sun*

Drinking

A Morning Coffee

Caffè Fiore
19 **F5**

A beloved Seattle coffee chainlet, Caffè Fiore serves incredible coffee, especially the sensational 'Sevvilla' – a mocha with orange zest. *6am-6pm*

Two Kick Coffee
20 **F2**

Coffee-lovers and bike aficionados alike will love Two Kick Coffee, with its incredible lattes and attached

motorcycle garage. *7am-7pm Mon-Wed, Fri & Sat, 7am-7:30pm Thu, 8am-5pm Sun*

Beers & Brews

Queen Anne Beerhall
21 **F6**

Local and imported European beers are the star of the show at Queen Anne Beerhall. Pair your ice-cold drink with a housemade pretzel and sausage platter to complete the German-inspired experience. *10:30am-midnight Mon-Thu, 10:30am-2am Fri, 11am-2am Sat & Sun*

Holy Mountain Brewing Company
22 **D5**

Holy Mountain has developed a serious cult following. Focused on ales aged in oak barrels and an ever-changing lineup of new taps, Holy Mountain offers beer-lovers a taste of something a bit different. *2-10pm Mon-Thu, noon-10pm Fri-Sun*

Figurehead Brewing
23 **C1**

Grab an ice-cold, locally brewed beer at this Magnolia brewing company. Add the rotating food trucks to the mix, and you can

make a full meal of your visit. *3-9pm Mon-Thu, 2-9pm Fri, noon-9pm Sat, 1-7pm Sun*

Shopping

Creative Arts

Queen Anne Book Company
24 **F4**

This charming little nook is everything a neighborhood bookstore should be, with frequent poetry readings and book signings. *10am-6pm Mon-Fri, to 5pm Sat & Sun*

Royal Records
25 **F5**

This unassuming record store is filled to the absolute max with vinyls – and cassettes, CDs, laserdiscs and VHS tapes. It also has quite an impressive international music section. *11am-7pm*

Blue Highway Games
26 **F4**

Blue Highway Games is home to just about every board game under the sun. Purchase your all-time favorite or opt for a PNW-themed one as a cool souvenir. *10am-9pm Sun-Thu, to 11pm Fri & Sat*

See p105
for eating,
drinking and
shopping
listings

Explore
Capitol Hill

Northeast of Downtown, Capitol Hill is a vibrant and progressive neighborhood celebrated for its diverse community, artistic spirit and thriving nightlife. Since the 1950s it has been a cornerstone of Seattle's LGBTIQ+ community, and by the 1990s it stood at the heart of the city's influential grunge scene. In the decades since, Capitol Hill has remained committed to inclusivity – a value that's visible in countless ways, from accessibility-focused reads on bookstore shelves to massive pride parades. Spend some time wandering through its thrift stores, independent cafes and music venues – you'll quickly feel the welcoming energy that defines Capitol Hill.

Getting Around

 **Light Rail & Streetcar**
There's one light rail station in Capitol Hill, aptly eponymously named. There are also two First Hill Streetcar stations: Broadway & Denny and Broadway Pike-Pine.

 Bus
Since the light rail and streetcar stops are relatively limited, buses are an essential part of getting around Capitol Hill. There are also direct buses between Capitol Hill and Downtown Seattle.

 Rideshare
Rideshares are an efficient way to get around the neighborhoods without having to deal with the hassle and cost of parking.

Starbucks Reserve Roastery (p104)
ARTCHEMY LABS/SHUTTERSTOCK

★

THE BEST

INCLUSIVE BOOKSTORE
Elliott Bay Book Company (p101)

COFFEE SHOP
Espresso Vivace (p106)

CLASSIC LGBTIQ+ HANGOUT
Pony (p103)

ON-THE-WATER ACTIVITY
Wild Haus Floating Saunas (p104)

HIGH-END TASTING MENU
Surrell (p106)

WALKING TOUR

An Appreciation of Capitol Hill's Art Scene

Capitol Hill has long been known as one of the artsiest neighborhoods in Seattle – and it goes beyond the visual arts. Sure, you'll find a good number of art galleries, but there are also countless bookstores and record stores, live theaters and music venues, solidifying its reputation as a cultural epicenter.

START	END	LENGTH
Wall of Sound	Elliott Bay Book Company	0.3 miles; 15min

1 A Loaded Record Store

Wall of Sound *(wosound.com)* is an old stalwart of Capitol Hill's vinyl record stores. It's tiny but absolutely loaded with more obscure and unusual finds. Whether you're in the market for psychfolk or Japanoise, there's a good chance that you'll find a few records for your collection here.

2 Record Store Rummaging

While some record stores feel curated, **Zion's Gate Records** on Pike St is anything but, which is, of course, all part of the charm. Drop into this slightly unkempt gem on Pike St and get ready to pick through records in search of rare LPs and 45s.

3 A Boundary-Pushing Theater

The small-scale **Annex Theatre** *(annextheatre.org)* puts on the sorts of bold, innovative plays that you won't find anywhere else.

This fringe theater is where quirky pitches – like a show based on *Cheers* where all the people are animals, or a puppet show that tackles the concept of existential dread – have their chance to be brought to life on stage in their full glory, complete with masterful set designs and costumes to complete the vision.

4 A Hub for Artists

Part-art gallery, part-performance space and part bar, **Vermillion** *(vermillionseattle.com)* is one of the trendiest Capitol Hill art hubs. Creatives of all types have found their footing here, from visual artists trying figure drawing to writers doing book launches to DJs testing out their latest sets.

5 Live-Music Nights

A punk, hip-hop and alternative-music joint, **Neumos** *(neumos.com)* is one of Seattle's most revered small music venues.

Its storied list of former performers is too long to include, but if they're cool and passing through Seattle, they've probably played here. The audience space can get hot and sweaty, and even smelly, but that's rock and roll.

6 A Beloved Bookstore

Elliott Bay Book Company *(elliottbaybook.com)* offers more than 150,000 titles in a large, airy, wood-beamed space with cozy nooks that can inspire hours of serendipitous browsing.

On its shelves, you'll find many books geared to encourage inclusivity – from accessible yoga guides to Filipino children's stories. In addition, the staff recommendations and displays of books by local authors make this place extra special.

Bibliophiles will be further satisfied with regular book readings and signings.

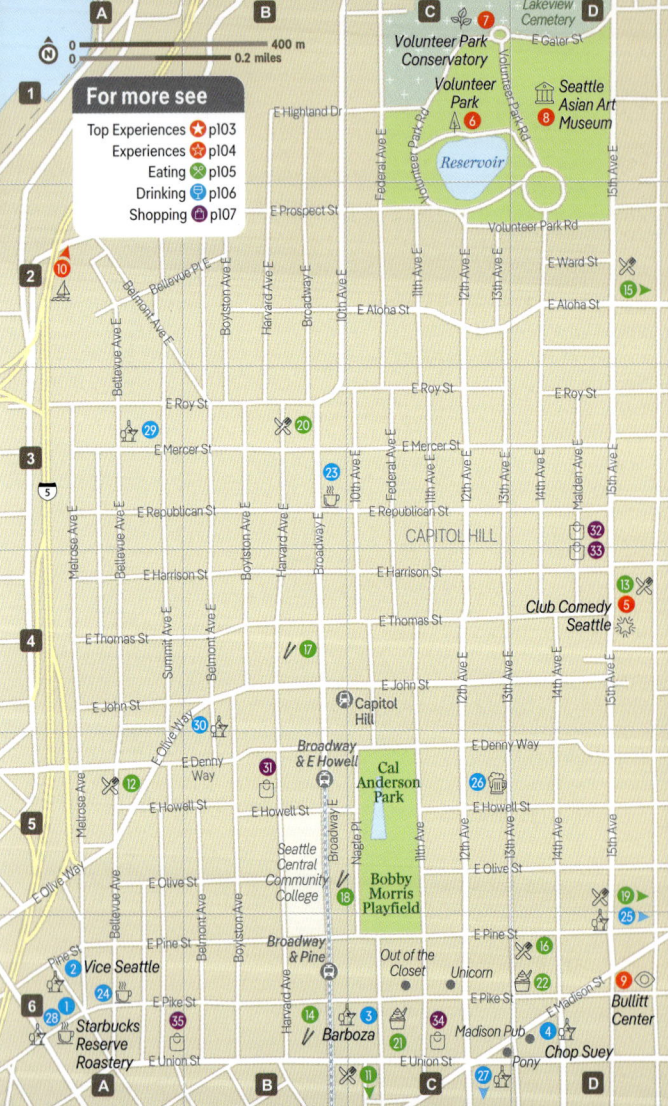

EXPLORE

CAPITOL HILL

For more see

Top Experiences ⭐ p103
Experiences ⭐ p104
Eating ✖ p105
Drinking 🍷 p106
Shopping 🛍 p107

Lakeview Cemetery

Volunteer Park Conservatory

Volunteer Park

Seattle Asian Art Museum

Reservoir

E Gater St

E Highland Dr

E Prospect St

Volunteer Park Rd

E Ward St

E Aloha St

E Roy St

E Roy St

E Mercer St

E Mercer St

CAPITOL HILL

E Republican St

E Republican St

E Harrison St

E Harrison St

E Thomas St

E Thomas St

Club Comedy Seattle

E John St

E John St

Capitol Hill

Broadway & E Howell

Cal Anderson Park

E Denny Way

E Denny Way

E Howell St

E Howell St

Seattle Central Community College

Bobby Morris Playfield

E Olive St

E Olive St

E Pine St

E Pine St

Vice Seattle

Broadway & Pine

Out of the Closet

Unicorn

Bullitt Center

Starbucks Reserve Roastery

Barboza

Madison Pub

Chop Suey

E Pike St

E Pike St

Pony

E Union St

E Union St

⭐ **TOP EXPERIENCE**

Capitol Hill's LGBTIQ+ Roots & Hot Spots

Pioneer Square (p57) used to be Seattle's LGBTIQ+ hub, but raising rents and redevelopment had the community relocating to Capitol Hill. As early as the 1950s, Capitol Hill established its reputation as an LGBTIQ+ hub, one with inclusive, affordable housing and all sorts of LGBTIQ+-focused businesses.

Seattle Pride

For a single day each June, Capitol Hill goes all out to celebrate the LGBTIQ+ community during **Seattle PrideFest**. (The festivities also include a second day at Seattle Center.) Spend the day shopping from queer vendors, eating from Seattle's best food trucks, watching talented LGBTIQ+ performances – from DJs to drag-show divas – and befriending other members of the community.

LGBTIQ+ Hot Spots

Bars and clubs make up the heart of the scene. **Pony** *(ponyseattle.com)* has reached a level of popularity where most denizens of Seattle's LGBTIQ+ nightlife scene either absolutely love or loathe it. The circus-themed **Unicorn** *(unicornseattle.com)* thrives both by night and by day, hosting a lively club atmosphere with jello shots and pinball games until late into the night, then a drag Sunday buffet brunch hours later. Let's not forget **Madison Pub** *(madisonpub.com)*, a gay sports bar, and **Wildrose** *(thewildrosebar.com)*, a long-time lesbian bar. Beyond the nightlife, the thrift store **Out of the Closet** *(outofthecloset.org)* donates proceeds toward AIDS research. Need a sweet treat? The fluffy, vegan donuts at **Dough Joy** (p106); *(doughjoydonuts.com)* are sure to please.

PLANNING TIP
While gay bars and clubs tend to be the most commonly recognized queer spaces, remember to explore Capitol Hill's other LGBTIQ+-friendly businesses – from boutiques to restaurants to theaters.

Check out EverOut's events schedule for the latest LGBTIQ+ happenings.

EXPERIENCES

Tour the Starbucks Reserve Roastery
FOOD & DRINK

MAP: **1** P102 **A6**

At the **Starbucks Reserve Roastery** (*starbucksreserve.com/locations/seattle-roastery*) in Capitol Hill, you can sip on coffee-tasting flights, get a behind-the-scenes look at the roasting area, take an espresso martini–making class and more.

Experience the Best of Capitol Hill's Nightlife Scene
NIGHTLIFE

For after-dark entertainment in Capitol Hill, pick your venue based on the music genre. **Vice Seattle** (MAP: **2** P102 **A6**; *viceseattle.com*) is known for EDM, **Barboza** (MAP: **3** P102 **C6**; *thebarboza.com*) has an eclectic but pop-heavy line-up, and the bookings at **Chop Suey** (MAP: **4** P102 **D6**; *chopsuey.com*) are as mixed as the dish it's named after.

Swap bass drops for punch lines with a night at **Club Comedy Seattle** (MAP: **5** P102 **D4**; *clubcomedyseattle.com*), which features both national headlines and up-and-coming local artists.

Enjoy the Gems of Volunteer Park
PARK

Volunteer Park (MAP: **6** P102 **C1**; *seattle.gov/parks/allparks/volunteer-park*) is a lovely green space with views of the Space Needle, with additional attractions tucked between the trees.

Admire the tropical plants in the **Volunteer Park Conservatory** (MAP: **7** P102 **C1**; *volunteerparkconservatory.com; adult/child $6/4*), then learn about East and South Asian art at the **Seattle Asian Art Museum** (MAP: **8** P102 **D1**; *seattleartmuseum.org/visit/seattle-asian-art-museum; adult/child $15/free*).

Tour the Sustainable Bullitt Center
TOUR

MAP: **9** P102 **D6**

Opened in 2013, the **Bullitt Center** (*bullittcenter.org*) is a beacon of sustainability. Designed according to the stringent 'Living Building' standards, this commercial office building takes the best sustainable practices – locally sourced materials, solar panels, and computer-operated windows and blinds – to create a net-positive energy building. Explore this building of the future on one of its biweekly **tours** (*$10*).

Take to Lake Union with Wild Haus Floating Saunas
WATER ACTIVITY

MAP: **10** P102 **A2**

Just outside of Capitol Hill proper, take to the shores of East Lake Union in one of the most unique ways around – via a floating sauna! These wood-fired **sauna boats** (*thewildhaus.com; from $150*) are as relaxing as it gets, heating your worries away as you sail on the lake and take in the city views.

Best Places for...

$ Budget $$ Midrange $$$ Top End

See p102 for map of locations

Eating

Pacific Northwest Flavors

Taylor Shellfish Oyster Bar $$

see A6

There's no better place to get oysters in Seattle than at Taylor's. There are a few locations throughout the city, but the Capitol Hill one is the flagship. If you're feeling adventurous, try the geoduck. *noon-8pm Sun-Thu, to 9pm Fri & Sat*

Lark Restaurant $$$

11 C6

Lark Restaurant is committed to showcasing local and seasonal PNW flavors with the help of the region's wonderful local purveyors. Mushrooms and seafood are often the name of the game. Order à la carte or splurge on a four-course tasting menu. *5-9pm Mon-Sat*

Flavor-Packed Takeout

Yalla $

12 A5

Alongside Seattle teriyaki (p119) and Dick's burgers (p119), Yalla is slowly becoming a go-to spot for to-go meals, with its crave-worthy Middle Eastern wraps and mezze accoutrements. *noon-10pm Mon-Thu, to midnight Fri-Sun*

Spice Waala $

13 D4

Like Yalla, Spice Waala is ingraining itself in the Capitol Hill take-out scene, this time with its bold, Indian street food. Try the *aloo tikka chaat* and the chicken *tikka kathi* rolls. *5-9pm Tue-Sat, plus 11am-2:30pm Wed-Sat*

Cozy Asian Eats

Ooink $

14 B6

Warm up with a comforting bowl of ramen at Ooink. While you can go with a classic shoyu or shio ramen, don't be afraid to go out-of-the-box, like with the spicy, pork-based mala ramen. *11:30am-9pm Sun-Thu, to 11pm Fri & Sat*

Taurus Ox $$

15 D2

Enjoy arguably the best Laotian food in the city through dishes like *thom khem* (pork-belly stew) and Lao sausage. *noon-9pm Tue-Sat*

Upscale Italian

Spinasse $$$

16 D6

Spinasse specializes in the cuisine of northern Italy's Piedmont region, particularly handmade and hand-cut pastas that are then coated in various ragù sauces. The finely curated wine list includes the best of the region's reds: Barolo and Barbaresco. *5-10pm Sun-Thu, to 11pm Fri & Sat*

Michelin-Worthy Sushi Spots

Taneda $$$

17 B4

With just nine seats, this Michelin-worthy sushi restaurant is nearly impossible to get into. If you do, an artful and seasonal multi-course *omakase* (chef's choice) experience awaits. *5:15-9:30pm Wed-Sun*

Ltd Edition Sushi 💲💲💲
18 B5

Believed to be one of the best Seattle restaurants, this eight-seat sushi eatery prioritizes seasonality in its *omakase* experience. If you want to splurge even more, consider the sake pairing. *5-9:30pm Mon-Fri*

High-End Tasting Menus
Surrell 💲💲💲
19 D5

Tucked in an unassuming house, a meal at Surrell feels like you've been invited into a wildly successful professional chef's home. Savor multiple courses of delicious food, all created with seasonal ingredients. Pescatarian, vegan and vegetarian options available. *6-9pm Wed-Sat*

Altura 💲💲💲
20 B3

Settle in for a three-hour dinner of small Italian plates made with seasonal ingredients. Though the menu is always changing, past dishes like saffron orecchiette and dry-aged duck breast showcase the caliber of dishes at Altura. *6-10pm Tue-Thu, 5-11pm Fri & Sat, 5-8pm Sun*

Vegan Sweets
Frankie & Jo's 💲
21 C6

Frankie & Jo's is a 100% vegan ice-cream shop in Capitol Hill that specializes in lux flavors such as chocolate tahini supercookie, beet strawberry rose and salty caramel ash, as well as made-from-scratch waffle cones. *4-10pm Mon-Fri, 1-10pm Sat & Sun*

Dough Joy 💲
22 D6

Satisfy your dessert cravings with the fluffy donuts from Dough Joy. This LGBTIQ+-owned spot offers incredible flavors – while still keeping everything on the menu completely vegan. There are also gluten-free donut options available. *8am-2pm Wed, Thu & Sun, to 9pm Fri & Sat*

Drinking

Coffee Shops
Espresso Vivace
23 B3

Espresso Vivace is widely regarded as serving up the best espresso in the city. As if that weren't enough, the founder David Schomer is credited with bringing latte art to the US. *6am-7pm*

Victrola Coffee Roasters
24 A6

Purveyors of fine cups o' coffee since 2000, Victrola is known for its 4oz cappuccinos that are as small as they are delicious. *6am-7pm*

Wine & Beer
Cagette
25 D6

This emerald wine bar has a classy, curated list of wines from France, Spain, the US and New Zealand. Enjoy small bites like pastries and sausages as you sip your red or white of choice. *4:30-9:30pm Tue & Wed, 9am-2pm Thu-Sun, plus 5-9:30pm Thu-Sat*

Outer Planet Craft Brewing
26 C5

This Capitol Hill nano-brewery makes its own European-inspired stouts, lagers, ales and sours. Add the fun board-game collection to the mix, and you've got yourself a great night out. *4-10pm Mon-Fri, 2-10pm Sat & Sun*

Well-Crafted Cocktails

Canon
 27 **C6**

Frequently listed as one of the best bars in the world, Canon has a spirit library that covers its walls several times over. Talented bartenders turn these spirits into innovative cocktails that are as tasty as they are artful. *5pm-1am Wed, Thu & Sun, to 2am Fri & Sat*

Rumba
 28 **A6**

The expansive collection of over 200 rums is the star of the show at this Caribbean-inspired bar. Sample your fair share with a rum flight, or single in on a Rumba Original craft cocktail. *5pm-midnight Mon-Thu, 4pm-midnight Fri-Sun*

Sol Liquor Lounge
 29 **A3**

Tucked away in a quieter part of the neighborhood, Sol Liquor Lounge has a bit of an old-school tiki-bar feel. *5pm-2am*

Doctor's Office
 30 **B4**

This doctor's office is way more fun than your typical PCP visit (though fun fact, this cocktail bar is actually owned by a doctor). Here, your 'prescription' is a masterfully crafted cocktail of your choice. *4pm-1am*

Shopping

Books on Books

Twice Sold Tales
 31 **B5**

This used bookstore has thousands of titles for all genres – and quite a few live-in cats. *11am-8pm*

Ada's Technical Books & Cafe
32 **D3**

This bookstore has a well-curated collection of self-proclaimed 'geeky' books on one side and a cafe on the other. Relax at the cafe tables or on a comfy chair in front of an old-fashioned fireplace. *8am-8pm*

A Closet Refresh

Creature Consignment
33 **D4**

This Capitol Hill consignment shop has racks filled with high-quality pieces from amazing brands. *10am-7pm Tue-Sun*

Glasswing
see **2** **A6**

Tucked in the small Melrose Market shopping and dining center, Glasswing is part clothing store, part plant shop, with cool vibes all around. *11am-6pm*

Curated Boutiques

Butter Home
34 **C6**

Located within the trendy Chophouse Row retail space, Butter Home is known for its adorable yet quirky home decor. Think butter-on-toast candle holders and handmade pickle-jar-shaped ornaments. *11am-6pm*

Standard Goods
35 **A6**

An expertly compiled selection of trendy clothing, comedic greeting cards and artsy mugs awaits at this Capitol Hill boutique. *noon-7pm Sun-Fri, to 8pm Sat*

See p119 for eating, drinking and shopping listings

Explore
North Seattle

A hop, skip and a bridge crossing from the heart of the city lies North Seattle. Separated from Queen Anne and Capitol Hill by several connected bodies of water, North Seattle is made up of a handful of distinct neighborhoods. There's Ballard, a historically seafaring community that's now one of the trendiest spots around, with its buzz-worthy restaurants and countless microbreweries. Next door in Fremont is where things get quirky – you'll find troll sculptures under bridges and whimsically curated gift shops. In Green Lake, you'll find an outdoorsy, active community, all centered on the eponymous lake, while the bustling University District – or U-District – is made for college kids, with well-connected public transport and affordable eats.

Getting Around

 Bus

Buses are your best bet in North Seattle, with countless routes criss-crossing through the neighborhoods. To determine the best route for you, use the Transit Go app (p35).

Light Rail

The light rail in North Seattle mostly services the U-District, with two stops in the one neighborhood. There's also one additional light rail stop – Roosevelt – closer to Green Lake.

Rideshare

Rideshares aren't a bad option in North Seattle, especially since driving is far from ideal, given the small streets and extremely limited parking.

Washington Park Arboretum (p116)
CLAUDIA G COOPER/SHUTTERSTOCK

THE BEST

SPRINGTIME BLOOMS
Cherry blossoms at
the Quad at UW (p116)

WILD ANIMAL SIGHTINGS
Salmon runs at the
Ballard Locks (p114)

EXPERIMENTAL MICROBREWERY
Lucky Envelope Brewing (p113)

PUBLIC ART PIECE
Fremont Troll (p117)

FISH & CHIPS SPOT
Pacific Inn Pub (p119)

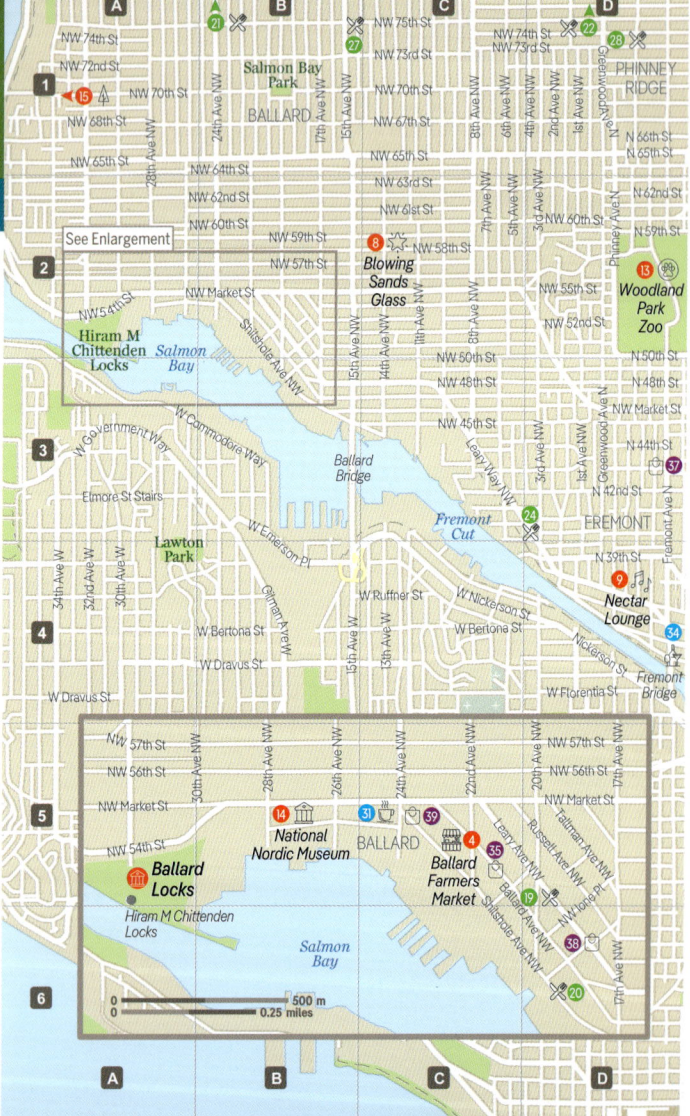

NW 74th St
NW 72nd St
NW 70th St
NW 68th St
NW 65th St

Salmon Bay Park

BALLARD

NW 75th St
NW 73rd St

NW 74th St
NW 73rd St

Greenwood

PHINNEY RIDGE

N 66th St
N 65th St

NW 64th St
NW 62nd St
NW 60th St
NW 59th St
NW 57th St

NW 63rd St
NW 61st St

NW 58th St
NW 55th St

N 62nd St
N 59th St

8 Blowing Sands Glass

13 Woodland Park Zoo

See Enlargement

NW 54th St
NW Market St

Hiram M Chittenden Locks

Salmon Bay

Shilshole Ave NW

NW 52nd St
NW 50th St
NW 48th St
NW 45th St

N 50th St
N 48th St
NW Market St
N 44th St
N 42nd St

37

W Government Way

W Commodore Way

Elmore St Stairs

Ballard Bridge

Fremont Cut

FREMONT

N 39th St

24

Lawton Park

W Emerson Pl

Gilman Ave NW

W Ruffner St

W Nickerson St

W Bertona St

9 Nectar Lounge

Nickerson St

34

W Bertona St

W Dravus St

W Dravus St

W Florentia St

Fremont Bridge

NW 57th St
NW 56th St
NW Market St
NW 54th St

NW 57th St
NW 56th St
NW Market St

Ballard Locks

Hiram M Chittenden Locks

14 National Nordic Museum

BALLARD

31

39

4 Ballard Farmers Market

35

19

Salmon Bay

38

20

0   500 m
0   0.25 miles

110

E **F** **G** **H**

NE 75th St

E Green Lake Dr N

NE 73rd St

1

5th Ave NE

Green Lake
Park **12**

NE 70th St

NE 68th St

28th Ave NE

25th Ave NE

Ravenna Ave NE

RAVENNA

36

23

NE 68th St

Green
Lake

NE 66th St

15th Ave NE

20th Ave NE

NE 65th St

N 65th St

NE 63rd St

NE 62nd St

NE 62nd St

W Green Lake Way N

Corliss Ave N

NE 61st St

East Green Lake Way N

NE 59th St

NE 58th St

Ravenna
Park

2

Woodland
Park

GREEN
LAKE

N 55th St

15th Ave NE

17th Ave NE

25th Ave NE

27th Ave NE

NE 55th St

NE 53rd St

NE 52nd St

U DISTRICT

N 52nd St

Meridian Ave N

Linden Ave N

Ashworth Ave N

Wallingford Ave N

NE 51st St

Roosevelt Way NE

NE 50th St

University
Village

NE 52nd St

N 50th St

3 U District
Farmers Market

16

N 47th St

NE 47th St

NE 45th St

NE 45th St

33

NE 45th St

3

N 45th St

Eastern Ave N

NE 44th St

17

NE 43rd St

26

N 43rd St

NE 43rd St

30

Quad

1

N 42nd St

NE 42nd St

N 41st St

Stone Way N

1st Ave NE

WALLINGFORD

N 40th St

NE Campus Pkwy

University of
Washington

Husky
Stadium

4

NE Pacific St

25

University
Bridge

N Pacific St

NE Pacific St

15th Ave NE

Montlake Blvd NE

Fremont
Troll

11

Agua Verde
Paddle Club **6**

University of
Washington

18

7

29

32

N 34th St

Fairview Ave E

Eastlake Ave E

UW Waterfront
Activities Center

2

Gas Works
Park

MONTLAKE

E Hamlin St

Lake
Union

E Roanoke St

Montlake
Park

E Roanoke St

E Calhoun St

WESTLAKE

EASTLAKE

E Lynn St

E Lynn St

Boyer Ave E

5

Dexter Ave N

Aurora Ave N

Fairview Ave E

E Galer St

24th Ave E

5

For more see

Top Experiences 🔴 p114
Experiences 🔴 p116
Eating 🟢 p119
Drinking 🔵 p120
Shopping 🟣 p121

Washington
Park
Arboretum

Galer St

E Highland Dr

MADISON
PARK

6

Prospect St

E Prospect St

Aloha St

Lake
Union
Park

1 km

0.5 miles

E **F** **G** **H**

WALKING TOUR

Ballard's Breweries & Cideries

The sheer number of breweries in Ballard has led to the well-deserved designation of a 'Ballard Brewery District'. Within a 1-mile radius, there are about a dozen craft breweries and cideries, each with its unique atmosphere and craft brews – from classic IPAs to innovative sours. It's safe to say that Ballard's behind-the-scenes brewers and cidermakers have created some exceptional products.

START	END	LENGTH
Bale Breaker & Yonder Cider Taproom	Channel Marker Cider	1.2 miles; 1hr

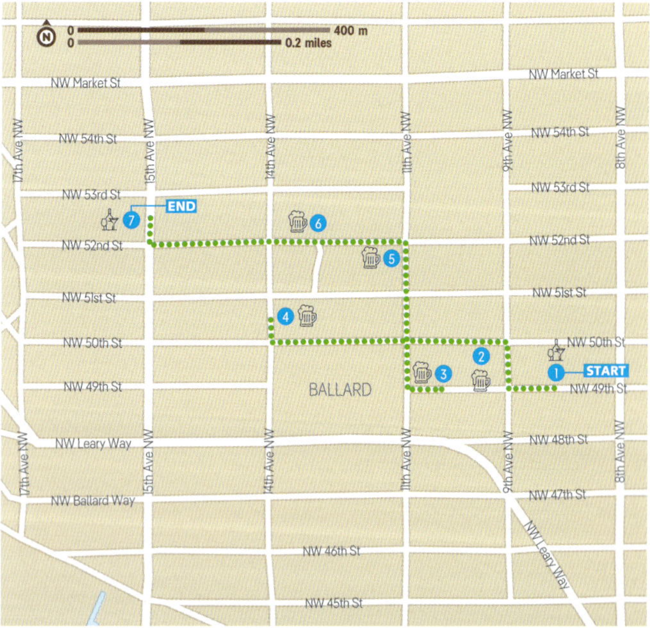

1 Two for One

At **Bale Breaker & Yonder Cider Taproom** (*bbycballard.com*), your choice is the beers of Bale Breaker or the ciders of Yonder Cider – and both are fantastic. The former leans into experimental, fruit-focused brews, while the latter leans heavily into the apple and pear flavors at its core.

2 Playing with Flavor

The brewers at **Lucky Envelope Brewing** (*luckyenvelopebrewing. com*) aren't afraid to experiment. In the past, the brews on tap have featured all sorts of flavors, including gingerbread, Buddha's hand citrus, and a peanut butter–cocoa-coffee blend.

3 Foraged & Farmhouse-Style

Fair Isle Brewing (*fairislebrewing. com*) aims to make all of its farmhouse-style beers with local ingredients – both to reflect the beauty of the PNW and because they're just that high quality. Flavors like berries and cherries pop up frequently, with some ingredients like elderflower and fireweed being foraged by the team (and their friends).

4 A Ballard Brewing OG

The family-owned **Reuben's Brews** (*reubensbrews.com*) was one of the first breweries in Ballard. Order your beer of choice from its ever-rotating list at a counter inside, where you can see the massive fermentation tanks at work. Then, take your beer out to the patio for some picnic tables, Seattle summer sunshine and food-truck eats.

5 Skilled in Sours

While **Urban Family Brewing Co** (*urbanfamilybrewing.com*) crafts all types of beer, it has made a name for itself in the world of sours, and it's embraccd it. Not only has it upped its sour-creation game, it also hosts a monthly comedy show called the Sour Hour, so you can enjoy some laughs with your drinks.

6 Czech Mate

Down the block, **Obec Brewing** (*obecbrewing.com*) specializes in European-style beers. While it makes brews from all over the continent – from England to Belgium – its Czech-style beers have stolen the show. Its malty Czech pilsner – which just so happens to be Obec Brewing's flagship beer – is definitely worth a try.

7 Crisp Ciders

Channel Marker Cider (*channel markercider.com*) is the only dedicated cider taproom in the Ballard Brewery District, and it's safe to say that its ciders are top-notch. Made with PNW apples, that crisp freshness comes through in every sip – even with boundary-pushing flavors like habanero lime and lavender bergamot. Not sure which cider is for you? Build your own cider flight for $4 per reasonably sized taster.

★ **TOP EXPERIENCE**

Ballard Locks

Seattle shimmers like an impressionist painting on sunny days at the Ballard Locks – officially called the Hiram M Chittenden Locks. Here, the fresh water of Lake Washington and Lake Union drops 22ft into salt water Puget Sound, a constructed phenomenon that has both boats and salmon rising with the waters.

MAP P110 **A5**

PLANNING TIP
To prevent harbor seals from hunting the salmon at the locks, the site has a loud, siren-esque system to scare these seals away. So don't be frightened when you hear it – keep watch for seals instead!

Scan for for a Ballard Locks sailing excursion with Argosy Cruises.

Watch the Boats Rise & Fall

The fundamental purpose of any lock system is to connect bodies of water with different elevations. In Ballard, it has the added bonus of (sort of) separating the salt water of Puget Sound with the fresh water of Lake Union and Lake Washington.

To then transfer boats between the high and low water levels – a 22ft difference – the locks act as a 'water elevator' of sorts. Stand inches away and watch the boats rise or sink (depending on direction) in just a matter of minutes! If you happen to be taking one of the many Seattle boat tours – like the **Argosy Cruises Locks Cruise** (*argosycruises.com/argosy-cruises/locks-cruise; adult/child $63/29*) – you could actually be on one of the boats and experience the rising and falling for yourself.

Catch the Salmon 'Run'

As if the 22ft water elevator of sorts wasn't enough, the Ballard Locks are a hot spot for salmon migration. From May to September, thousands of salmon swim and jump their way upstream via the fish ladder on the southern side of the locks, in the hopes of making it to fresh water to spawn. Watch them pop out of the

VDB PHOTOS/SHUTTERSTOCK

water in the blink of an eye, or head into the underwater viewing gallery to get a glimpse of the salmon who have made it across safely.

The Ballard Locks Visitor Center & Museum

The small but informative **Ballard Locks Visitor Center, Museum & Gift Shop** is a great place to end your experience. After all, now that the boats and salmon have gotten your attention, it's the perfect opportunity to learn about the science and engineering behind the structure. Take your time strolling through the exhibits, which explain everything from the hydraulic principles governing the lock system to the innovative design of the fish ladder.

TAKE A BREAK
Take a seat at a bench at the often-overlooked **Carl S English Jr Botanical Garden**, a small botanical garden lining the northern section of the locks.

EXPERIENCES

Stop & Smell the Cherry Blossoms in the UW Quad   GARDEN

MAP: **1** P110 **H3**

Each spring, the 29 Yoshino cherry trees in the **Quad at UW** (*washington.edu/cherryblossoms*) bloom with pale pink and white cherry blossom flowers. Add the green, manicured landscaping and historic brick buildings to the mix, and the whole area is absolutely stunning. Since the cherry blossoms only stick around for a couple of weeks – usually late March to mid-April – expect lots of other flower admirers during your visit.

Watch the Sunset from Gas Works Park   PARK

MAP: **2** P110 **E4**

For a scenic spot to enjoy a picnic or let out some energy on a playground while enjoying stunning views of the city, visit **Gas Works Park** (*seattle.gov/parks/allparks/gas-works-park*). This former gas plant turned park offers plenty of green space, as well as picturesque views of Lake Union and the Seattle skyline.

Shop the Local Farmers Market Scene   FARMERS MARKET

There are lovely farmers markets dotted all around the city, but there are two particularly noteworthy ones in North Seattle: the **U District Farmers Market** (MAP: **3** P110 **G2**; *seattlefarmersmarkets.org/udfm*) and the **Ballard Farmers Market** (MAP: **4** P110 **C5**; *sfmamarkets*

.com/visit-ballard-farmers-market). With the former on Saturday mornings and the latter on Sunday mornings, you can spend your whole weekend perusing local finds – from fresh organic produce to warm bread loaves to blooming flower bouquets.

Kayak to the Washington Park Arboretum   BOTANICAL GARDEN

Across the water in nearby Madrona, the free-to-visit **Washington Park Arboretum** (MAP: **5** P110 **H5**; *botanicgardens.uw.edu/washington-park-arboretum*) thrives with over 40,000 plants across its 230 acres. While you can walk these lush grounds, you can also explore them via kayak. Rent one from **Agua Verde Paddle Club** (MAP: **6** P110 **G4**; *aguaverdepaddleclub.com; per hr from $24*) or the **UW Waterfront Activities Center** (MAP: **7** P110 **H4**; *washington.edu/ima/waterfront; per hr from $21*), both in the University District. Then paddle between Marsh and Foster Island, circling the latter of the two for a peaceful, greenery-filled experience.

Take a Class at Blowing Sands Glass   ART CLASS

MAP: **8** P110 **C2**

Some say that Seattle has a metaphorical heart of glass, given the many glass shops and glass-blowing studios dotted throughout

LOOKING FOR MORE TROLLS?

If you thought the greater Seattle area could only have one troll sculpture, well, you'd be wrong. In addition to the Fremont Troll, there are a handful of others spread around, all made by Danish environmental artist Thomas Dambo. Find these trolls in Ballard, West Seattle, Bainbridge Island, Vashon Island and Issaquah (the final one is in the PNW series in Portland, Oregon), tucked amid the trees or standing proudly in front of museums. Learn more about these incredible sculptures and the artist behind them at *nwtrolls.org*.

the city – as well as the famed Chihuly Garden and Glass (p78) in Seattle Center, of course. So it's safe to say that there's no better place to try glass blowing than in Seattle. Ballard's **Blowing Sands Glass** (*blowingsands.com*) offers well-priced, beginner glass-blowing classes (starting at $45), during which you can make anything from an ornament to a sea star to a vase.

Listen to Live Music at Nectar Lounge
MUSIC VENUE

MAP: **9** P110 **D4**

This small and comfortable **live-music venue** (*nectarlounge.com*) in Fremont outgrew its humble beginnings to become a well-established club that includes a covered patio with stage views. It prides itself on hosting any genre of music and was an early refuge for hip-hop acts. Macklemore and Wiz Khalifa have both played here.

Swap Tailgating for Sailgating
SPORTS

MAP: **10** P110 **H4**

You've heard of tailgating before a sports game, but what about sailgating? Since the University

of Washington's **Husky Stadium** (*gohuskies.com*) is right on Lake Washington's Union Bay, it's popular for the most avid football fans to charter a boat, join a sailgating cruise, or even take out their own vessel, dropping anchor a little ways away from the shore and reveling in pre-game food, drinks and fun. To get to the stadium, you'll need to flag down the shuttle boat service – they start getting crowded about an hour before the start of the game – and they'll get you where you need to go.

Pay a Visit to the Fremont Troll
PUBLIC ART

MAP: **11** P110 **E4**

Beneath the Aurora Bridge sprouts the **Fremont Troll**, a 13,000lb steel-and-concrete sculpture of a troll crushing a Volkswagen Beetle that guards the neighborhood. The sculpture was made by a group of four artists – Steve Badanes, Will Martin, Donna Walter and Ross Whitehead – and it was the winner of a 1989 Fremont Arts Council competition to design some thought-provoking public art.

Wander Around Green Lake PARK

MAP: **12** P110 **F1**

A favorite hunting ground for runners, personal trainers and artistically tattooed sunbathers, scenic **Green Lake Park** (seattle.gov/parks/allparks/green-lake-park) surrounds a small natural lake created by a glacier during the last ice age. The paths that wind around the lake are usually well used by those on foot and wheels of every variety, and make for some of the best people- (and dog-) watching in the city.

Make a Few Animal Friends at Woodland Park Zoo ZOO

MAP: **13** P110 **D2**

The **Woodland Park Zoo** (zoo.org; adult/child from $27/16) is one of Seattle's most popular tourist attractions and is consistently rated as one of the top 10 zoos in the country. It was one of the first in the nation to free animals from their restrictive cages in favor of ecosystem enclosures, where animals from similar environments share large spaces designed to replicate their natural surroundings. Say hello to the beloved red pandas and Humboldt penguins while you're there!

Learn About Ballard's Scandinavian Roots MUSEUM

MAP: **14** P110 **B5**

Reason enough to come to North Seattle – if the brewery scene and waterfront parks weren't enough –

the **National Nordic Museum** (nordicmuseum.org; adult/child $20/10) is a delightful surprise. Dedicated to Nordic history and culture, this museum is now housed in a fjord-inspired building and features incredible permanent exhibits on Nordic Journeys, spanning 12,000 years of Nordic life, culture and immigration to North America, as well as the monumental Project Aurora installation. The temporary exhibits, while usually requiring a minimal additional entry fee, are more than worth the few extra bucks to dive into lesser-known Scandinavian stories, artifacts, artwork and more.

Soak up the Sun at Golden Gardens Park BEACH

MAP: **15** P110 **A1**

Golden Gardens Park (seattle.gov/parks/allparks/golden-gardens-park) is a serene and stunning beach park where you can bask in the breathtaking views of Puget Sound and Olympic Mountains. The park has a clean and well-kept sandy beach, fire pits, a playground and a casual food stand open during summer, when the beach is filled with people picnicking, playing volleyball or just taking in the views. But parking spots are hard to come by. While the cold waters of Puget Sound might feel good on the hottest of summer days, it borders on being too cold for most, so brace yourself!

Best Places for...

$ Budget $$ Midrange $$$ Top End

See p110 for map of locations

Eating

Seattle Institutions

Toshi's Teriyaki $

16 H3

There's a saying in Seattle – Japan created teriyaki, but Seattle perfected it – and much of that perfection is due to Toshi's Teriyaki, which is a Seattle institution. Toshi's puts a slight variation on the traditional style, adding punchy ginger and garlic. *11am-8pm Mon-Sat*

Dick's Drive-In $

17 F3

Ask any Seattleite where to get a burger, and there's a good chance they'll tell you about Dick's. Visit its original location in Wallingford – opened in 1954 – where it continues to sling out tasty, affordable burgers and build its cult following. *10:30am-2am*

Seafood Staples

Pacific Inn Pub $$

18 E4

There are a lot of opinions about where to get the best fish and chips in Seattle, and Pacific Inn Pub gets its fair share of votes. The spiced, panko-crusted coating makes the dish. *11am-2am*

MacLeod's Scottish Pub $$

19 D5

If you're looking for more classic UK beer-battered fish and chips, MacLeod's is your spot. It's also known for its single malt whiskies and scotch cocktails. *4-11pm Wed & Thu, to 2am Fri & Sat, 2-10pm Sun*

Walrus and the Carpenter $$

20 D6

Puget Sound waters practically bleed oysters and – arguably – there isn't a better place to knock 'em back raw with a glass of wine or two than the Walrus and the Carpenter. The accolades (like the customers) keep flying in. *4-9pm Sun-Thu, to 10pm Fri & Sat*

Only the Highest-Quality Meats

Peasant $$$

21 B1

By day, this venue is Beast and Cleaver butcher shop; by night (or, more accurately, evening), it turns into the Peasant, a contemporary eatery that uses seasonal ingredients and high-quality meats for its ever-changing menu. *7:30-10pm Thu & Fri*

FlintCreek Cattle Co $$$

22 D1

FlintCreek Cattle Co uses only the highest-quality meats from small-scale ranches. While its mains can get pricey, visit for daily happy hour *(4pm to 5:30pm at the bar)* for the incredible $11 Butcher Burger. *4-10pm*

Award-Worthy Experiences

Wataru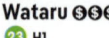

23 H1

Using a combination of local seafood and fish flown in from Tokyo's famed Toyosu Fish Market, Wataru crafts an incredible *edomae*-style, sushi-heavy *omakase* for its limited number of diners. *7:30-10pm Wed, 5-10pm Thu & Fri, 4:30-10pm Sat & Sun*

Hamdi 🄢🄢🄢

24 D3

Preparing Turkish food at its finest, Hamdi is known for its lamb-based kebap (an elevated play on a casual kebab) and its wildly avant-garde cocktails. *5-9pm Thu-Sun*

Kamonegi 🄢🄢🄢

25 E4

Kameonegi specializes in soba noodles and tempura, with many vegetarian options for plant-based diners. The restaurant feels refreshingly authentic, down to its Tokyo side-street-sized dining area. Reservations recommended. *4-9:30pm Tue-Sat*

Casual Eats

Off the Rez Cafe 🄢

26 G3

Tucked inside the Burke Museum, Off the Rez introduces Native American flavors to the Seattle culinary scene, with its fry-bread tacos and wild-rice bowls. *10am-5pm Tue-Sun*

Un Bien 🄢

27 B1

Lines can get long at this family-owned Caribbean take-out spot, but the wait is worth it to finally sink your teeth into a perfectly juicy and tangy pork sandwich. *11am-9pm Wed-Sat, to 8pm Sun*

Southeast Asian Restaurants

Sophon 🄢🄢

28 D1

Sophon serves as a wonderful introduction to the Khmer people – a Cambodian Indigenous group – and their cuisine. Its seasonal food menu features flavors like lime leaves and coconut milk, which pair perfectly with its innovative, often tropical, cocktails. *5-9pm Tue-Sat*

Drinking

Next-Level Coffee Experiences

Milstead & Co

29 E4

This fabulous Fremont coffee bar carefully selects its beans with the skill and precision of a French sommelier. The 'bean menu' changes daily, but, thanks to the expertise of owner Andrew Milstead, it rarely disappoints. *7am-4pm*

Cafe Allegro

30 G3

Claiming the title of Seattle's oldest continually operating coffee shop, this U-District cafe has long been a local – and visitor – favorite, with lattes made with house-roasted beans and a cozy atmosphere. *7am-5pm Mon-Fri, 8am-5pm Sat & Sun*

Cardoon

31 C5

A hidden gem of a cafe, Cardoon brings international flavors to its coffee and pastries. Try the seaweed latte with soy-sauce caramel and the Iranian-inspired chickpea-and-cardamom-based rose cookie. *8am-4pm Wed-Fri, Sun & Mon, to 8pm Sat*

Brewed & Vinified

Fremont Brewing
 32 E4

This microbrewery sells its wares via an attached tasting room rather than a full-blown pub. The beer is divine – try the seasonal barrel-aged bourbon Abominable – and the 'urban beer garden' is a wonderful place to sip. *11am-9pm*

Lad & Lass Brewing
33 G3

Owned and operated by a husband-and-wife team, this little U-District brewery and taproom crafts all sorts of beer styles – from pilsners to stouts. *3-9pm Wed & Thu, 3-10pm Fri, 2-10pm Sat, 2-8pm Sun*

Schilling Cider House
34 D4

Swap beer for hard cider – or a glass of hard lemonade – from both local and international purveyors at this Fremont tap room. *4-9pm Mon & Thu, 4-10pm Fri, noon-10pm Sat, noon-9pm Sun*

Shopping
Curated Gifts
LUCCA Great Finds
35 C5

The front half of this Ballard boutique is a chic PNW-themed homewares store that will have you redesigning your home. In the back is a stationery shop with enviably stylish wrapping paper and charming greeting cards. *11am-6pm Mon-Sat, 10am-5pm Sun*

Woodland Mod
see **35** C5

Cozy but modern, Woodland Mod is filled with must-have homewares. While you can't buy out the whole store, you can take a ceramic mug, a collection of greeting cards or a few bars of high-quality imported soaps. *11am-6pm Mon-Thu, 11am-7pm Fri & Sat, 10am-5pm Sun*

A Bookshelf Restock
Third Place Books
36 H1

Third Place Books is one of the most beloved bookstores in Seattle. Find your next read – new or used – then settle in with

a coffee from the cafe or a beer from the pub, both tucked inside. *9am-9pm*

Book Larder
37 D3

Book Larder isn't your average bookstore. As the name hints, this Fremont gem is all about cookbooks – new, used or vintage. It also frequently hosts both author signings and cooking classes. *11am-6pm Mon-Fri, 11am-5pm Sat, noon-4pm Sun*

Mox Boarding House
38 D6

It's all fun and games at Mox Boarding House, where board and card games dominate the scene. Grab a table at the bar-cafe and try out a new game from its eclectic 'library'. *11am-10pm Mon-Thu, 11am-midnight Fri, 10am-midnight Sat, 10am-10pm Sun*

Weirdly Wonderful
Ballyhoo
39 C5

Even if you think you've been to every oddities shop worth a two-headed calf, Ballyhoo is worth a visit. On one side you'll find fun trinkets in the $1 to $10 range and on the other, a fossilized woolly-mammoth tooth. *noon-7pm*

See p129
for eating,
drinking and
shopping
listings

Explore
South Seattle

South Seattle is made up of several different neighborhoods, including Georgetown, Beacon Hill, Rainier Valley and Seward Park. Though they're often grouped together under the larger South Seattle title for ease, each of these neighborhoods has its own distinct flair: Georgetown is historic and industrial, with a growing artistic side; the relatively quiet Beacon Hill is filled to the brim with under-the-radar food finds; Rainier Valley is a multicultural haven, with some of the best pan-African eateries in the city; and Seward Park is a nature-lover's dream, with Lake Union–front gems and large forest-filled green spaces.

Getting Around

 **Light Rail**
There are several light rail stops in this region: Beacon Hill, Mt Baker, Columbia City, Othello and Rainier Beach.

 Bus
From your light rail stop, you may need to take one of the many bus routes to reach your precise destination.

 Car
South Seattle may be one of the only regions in Seattle where driving isn't a bad option. The roads may still be squishy and pothole-filled and you'll have to pay for parking, but you at least will be able to find parking pretty easily.

Seward Park (p128)
KWAN TSE/SHUTTERSTOCK

THE BEST

GUAMANIAN CUISINE
familyfriend (p130)

ETHIOPIAN RESTAURANT
Alem Restaurant (p129)

ALTERNATIVE COMIC STORE
Fantagraphics Bookstore & Gallery (p127)

COZY LETTERPRESS PRINT SHOP
Day Moon Press (p131)

LAKEFRONT WALK
Seward Park Loop (p128)

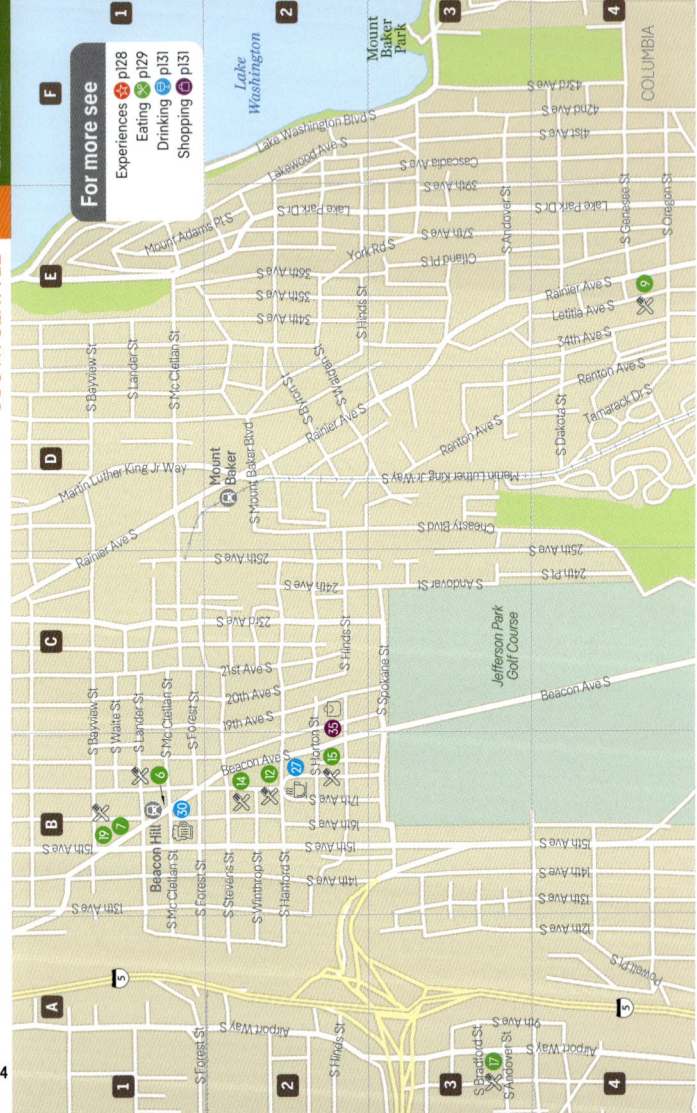

For more see

Experiences ✿ p128
Eating ✗ p129
Drinking 🍷 p131
Shopping 🛍 p131

Lake
Washington

Mount
Baker
Park

COLUMBIA

S 43rd Ave S
S 42nd Ave S
41st Ave S
Cascadia Ave S
39th Ave S
S Andover St
S Genesee St
S Oregon St

Lake Washington Blvd S
Lakewood Ave S
Lake Park Dr S

Mount Adams Pl S

York Rd S

Otland Pl S
36th Ave S
35th Ave S
34th Ave S

S Hinds St

Rainier Ave S
Letitia Ave S
34th Ave S

Renton Ave S

Lake Park Dr S

S Dakota St
Tamarack Dr S

S Bayview St
S Lander St
S McClellan St

Rainier Ave S

S Dakota St

Renton Ave S

Mount
Baker

Martin Luther King Jr Way

Mount Baker Blvd

Martin Luther King Jr Way S

Rainier Ave S

S 25th Ave S

S Andover St

Cheasty Blvd S

25th Ave S
24th Pl S

S Bayview St
S Waite St
S Lander St
S McClellan St
S Forest St

21st Ave S
20th Ave S
19th Ave S

24th Ave S
23rd Ave S

S Hinds St

S Spokane St

S Andover St

Jefferson Park
Golf Course

Beacon Ave S

Beacon Ave S

Beacon Hill

14th Ave S

15th Ave S
14th Ave S
13th Ave S
12th Ave S

S Horton St
35
15
27
12
14

S Plum St
17th Ave S
16th Ave S
15th Ave S
14th Ave S

S McClellan St
S Stevens St
S Winthrop St
S Hanford St

S Forest St

S Bradford St
S Andover St

Airport Way S

S Hinds St

9th Ave S

S Ferdinand St

Airport Way S

13th Ave S

6
7
19
30
17

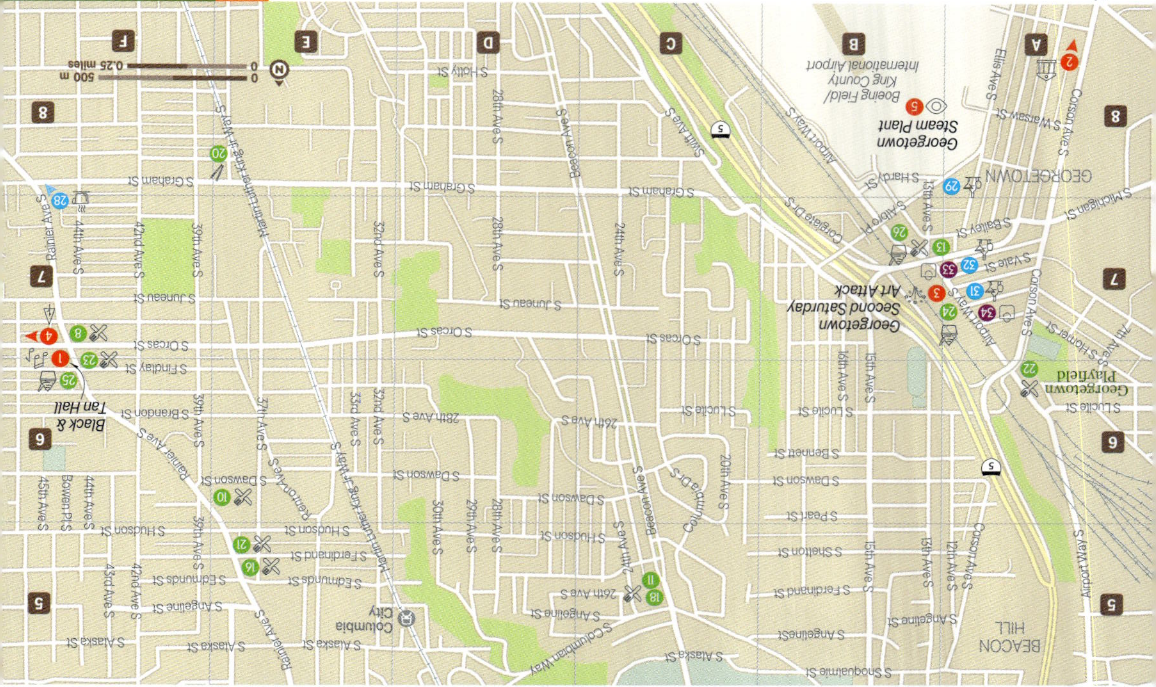

Georgetown Steam Plant
Boeing Field/ King County International Airport
Georgetown Second Saturday Art Attack
Black & Tan Hall
GEORGETOWN
BEACON HILL
Columbia City
Georgetown Playfield
Rainier Ave S
Martin Luther King Jr Way S
Beacon Ave S
Airport Way S
Swift Ave S
Corson Ave S
Renton Ave S
Columbia Dr S
S Columbian Way
Corgiate Dr S
S Graham St
S Orcas St
S Juneau St
S Findlay St
S Brandon St
S Dawson St
S Hudson St
S Ferdinand St
S Edmunds St
S Angeline St
S Alaska St
S Holly St
S Lucile St
S Bennett St
S Pearl St
S Shelton St
S Snoqualmie St
S Michigan St
S Bailey St
S Vale St
S Hardy St
S Warsaw St
S Homer St
Ellis Ave S
28th Ave S
24th Ave S
26th Ave S
32nd Ave S
33rd Ave S
37th Ave S
39th Ave S
42nd Ave S
43rd Ave S
44th Ave S
45th Ave S
Bowen Pl S
29th Ave S
30th Ave S
20th Ave S
16th Ave S
15th Ave S
13th Ave S
12th Ave S
7th Ave S
0 500 m
0 0.25 miles
A B C D E F
5 6 7 8

WALKING TOUR

Eat & Shop Your Way Through Georgetown

Georgetown has the makings of an up-and-coming trendy neighborhood, with its historic architecture, retro shops and hole-in-the-wall eateries. It's easy enough to wander around the neighborhood center (clustered along Airport Way, roughly between S Albro Pl and 8th Ave) on foot, popping into whatever businesses catch your eye.

START	END	LENGTH
Maruta Shoten	Matcha Man Ice Cream & Taiyaki	0.3 miles; 15min

1 A Bustling Japanese Market

A Georgetown epicenter, **Maruta Shoten** (*marutashoten.com*) is always bustling, but especially at lunch and just before its 6pm closing. Though relatively small, it's stocked to the brim with the best Japanese (and generally East Asian) ingredients. But the bigger draw is the deli, home to freshly made karaage, fried rice, shrimp tempura and more. There are also grab-and-go bento boxes with favorites like chicken katsu and sushi.

2 Tantalizing Tortas

You'll smell the tortas from **El Pirata Tortas Y Burritos** (*elpiratatortas.com*) before you clearly catch sight of this little brick building. There are half a dozen variations on this Mexican sandwich, but the El Cubano torta with its absurdly tender pork and the spicy Habanero chicken torta are two must-tries. Add a side of its popular mac salad for a great meal.

3 Vietnamese Eats

Around the corner, **Voi Cà Phê** (*voicaphe.com*) primarily serves up two Vietnamese favorites – banh mi and Vietnamese coffee – and has mastered them both. For the best experience, you'll want to order the iced condensed-milk phin coffee and the pork sausage patty banh mi (perhaps in the mini size if you're getting full). Just outside, you'll also find a couple of worn public benches where you can eat your food haul.

4 Alternative Comics Hot Spot

Fantagraphics Bookstore & Gallery (*fantagraphics.com/pages/fantagraphics-bookstore-gallery*), a local alternative publishing company, specializes in comics, graphic novels, classic comic-strip anthologies, manga and magazines – all of which can be found in its charming Georgetown retail store.

5 A Well-Curated Vintage Collection

Barn Owl Vintage Goods (*barnowlseattle.com*) is the ideal kind of vintage store. It's clean, well organized and well curated, with the vast majority of the items in the store looking like they could be brand new – and it surprisingly has a larger collection of men's items than women's. In addition to quality tees and Levi's jeans, there are a few fun oddities, like a large inventory of cowboy boots and quite a few denim and leather vests.

6 Ice Cream in a Fish-Shaped Cone

End your Georgetown walk at **Matcha Man Ice Cream & Taiyaki** with soft-serve ice cream in a fish-shaped, cake-esque cone. Keep it relatively simple with just ice cream – which comes in flavors like matcha, black sesame and ube – or treat yourself to a traditional red-bean filling to really round out the *taiyaki* experience.

EXPERIENCES

Listen to Live Music at the Black & Tan Hall   MUSIC VENUE

MAP: **1** P124 **F6**

Named for the famous Black-owned music club that thrived in Seattle from the 1930s for five decades, the inclusive **Black & Tan Hall** (blackandtanhall.com) in Hillman City pays homage to Black improvisational jazz culture, presenting music as well as cultural workshops and social-change events.

Explore the Museum of Flight   MUSEUM

MAP: **2** P124 **A8**

Chronicling flight history from Kitty Hawk to Concorde, the city that spawned Boeing unsurprisingly houses the **Museum of Flight** (museumofflight.org; adult/child $29/21), one of the nation's finest aviation museums. It's a multifarious affair that includes exhibits on some of the most ingenious gravity-defying human-made objects: picture nefarious V2 rockets, Apollo lunar modules and aerodynamic gliders.

Get Creative at the Second Saturday Art Attack   EVENT

MAP: **3** P124 **B7**

Georgetown's industrial art scene pulls together on the second weekend of each month at the **Georgetown Second Saturday Art Attack** (georgetownseattle.org/art-attack). This is the best time to visit the neighborhood's myriad galleries, some of which have rather sporadic opening hours. Almost the entire commercial strip takes part in this lively monthly event.

Walk the Waterfront Seward Park Perimeter Loop   HIKE

MAP: **4** P124 **F7**

Seward Park is a lovely little peninsula in Lake Union, one filled with towering trees and peaceful walking trails. For the best views of the water, circumnavigate the park via the 2.4-mile **Seward Park Perimeter Loop Trail** (wta.org/go-hiking/hikes/seward-park). On the clearest of days, you can even spot Mt Rainier from the south side of the park.

Take a Tour of the Georgetown Steam Plant   HISTORIC SITE

MAP: **5** P124 **B8**

The **Georgetown Steam Plant** (georgetownsteamplant.org) was built by the Seattle Electric Company in 1906 to power some of the city's streetcars. It stayed in service for 47 years, officially getting decommissioned two decades after that in 1972. Today, you can take a behind-the-scenes look at this historic, steampunk-esque site on the second Saturday of each month between 10am and 2pm, with free tours at 10:30am, 11:30am and 12:30pm.

Best Places for...

$ Budget $$ Midrange $$$ Top End

See p124 for map of locations

Eating

Filipino Finds

Chebogz $

6 B1

Chebogz serves up affordable Filipino comfort food with popular dishes like chicken adobo and *lumpia* (Filipino spring rolls). *11am-7:30pm Wed-Sat, to 5:30pm Sun*

Musang $$$

7 B1

Passed-down family recipes are reimagined as contemporary Filipino dishes (and cocktails) at this Beacon Hill restaurant. *5-10pm*

East African Eats

Delish Ethiopian Cuisine $$

8 F7

Run by a husband-and-wife team, this South Seattle Ethiopian restaurant is known for its expansive platters, each with small helpings of several stewy, often veggie-forward items and a side of injera (tangy flatbread). *4-9pm Sun, Mon & Wed-Fri, 1-9pm Sat*

Alem Restaurant $$

9 F4

Serving Habesha cuisine – a subset of Ethiopian and Eritrean food culture – Alem Restaurant's menu is filled with flavorful stews, aromatic meats and the always beloved injera. *10am-midnight*

Safari Njema Restaurant $

10 E6

Build your own Kenyan combo plate at this Rainier Ave restaurant, with dishes like *ugali* (cornmeal cake), *sukuma* (stewed greens), and whole fried fish. *11am-9pm Mon & Wed-Sat, 2-9pm Sun*

More than Excellent Pizza

Clock-Out Lounge $

11 C5

Clock-Out Lounge has a lot going for it: great drinks, even better pizza, live music and epic drag performances. *4-9pm Sun-Thu, to 10pm Fri & Sat*

Bar del Corso $$

12 B2

Bar del Corso has mastered the art of wood-fired pizzas. Devour one all on your own, or split it – and delicious small plates like grilled octopus and house-made meatballs – with friends. *4-9pm Tue-Sat*

Mediterranean & Middle Eastern

Cuidad $$$

13 B7

If it weren't for the aromatic Middle Eastern spice blends wafting through the air, it'd be easy to miss this incredibly delicious Georgetown hole-in-the-wall. *11:30am-9pm Sun-Thu, to 10pm Fri & Sat*

Homer $$$

14 B2

Right on Beacon Hill's main throughway, Homer is a popular spot for all things Mediterranean and Middle Eastern – from freshly baked pita with labneh (soft cheese dip) to anise hyssop (floral herb) soft serve. *5-10pm Tue-Sun*

Flavors from the Islands

familyfriend $$

15 B2

Despite having essentially no online presence, familyfriend has developed a cult-like following with its uniquely Guamanian flavors. *5-9:30pm*

Island Soul $$

16 E5

Feel transported to Jamaica – by way of the American South – with dishes like jerk-seasoned catfish po' boys and beef hotlink-based gumbo. *4-10pm Mon-Wed, 4pm-1am Thu, 4pm-midnight Fri, noon-midnight Sat*

Cozy Barbecue

Raney's Bar & Grill $$

17 A3

Whether you're hoping for brisket, ribs or wings, Raney's Bar & Grill can deliver some of the smokiest, fall-off-the-bone barbecue around. *11am-8pm Mon-Wed, to 9pm Thu & Fri*

Cheap Eats

Dim Sum House $

18 C5

The under-the-radar Dim Sum House is, without a doubt, the place to get dim sum in South Seattle – and at a great price, too. Try the pork siu mai, steamed bean curd rolls, and chicken feet. *9am-9pm Thu-Tue*

Carnitas Michoacan $

19 B1

Home to some of the best Mexican food in the city, Carnitas Michoacan's house-made corn tortillas, juicy carnitas and flavor-packed salsa make for some incredible tacos and burritos. *11am-9pm Mon-Fri, 10am-9pm Sat & Sun*

Rainier Restaurant $

20 E8

One of the most authentic Vietnamese restaurants in the city, Rainier Restaurant's homey dishes are so delicious that even food critic Anthony Bourdain loved them. *11am-11pm Sun-Thu, to midnight Fri & Sat*

Splurge-Worthy Meals

Off Alley $$$

21 E5

Tucked into what feels like an actual brick hallway, Off Alley has reinvented the concept of fine dining – with a casual atmosphere, punk rock music, and the best seasonal ingredients in an eight-course $200+ tasting menu. *5-9pm Thu & Sun, to 10pm Fri & Sat*

Corson Building $$$

22 A6

Dining at the Corson Building feels like you've been transported into a historic Mediterranean home, one where a fresh vegetable-forward menu will reignite your love for seasonal produce. *6-9pm Thu & Fri, 5:30-9:30pm Sat, 5:30-9pm Sun*

Archipelago Seattle $$$

23 F6

Pacific Northwest ingredients and Filipino flavors meet at this Michelin-worthy restaurant, where cultural appreciation and sustainable practices stay at the forefront. *hours vary*

Delectable Desserts

Fran's Chocolate $

24 A7

Take a look at the chocolate-making process of this beloved local company. Choco-holics, book the guided chocolate tasting. *10am-5pm Mon-Sat*

Flour Box $

25 F6

Prepare to stand in a line that curves around the block to get a taste of the Flour Box's fluffy, hand-piped brioche donuts. *10am-12:30pm Thu-Sun or until sold out*

Deep Sea Sugar and Salt **⑤**

 26 B7

If you're craving moist cakes in fun but classy flavors, there's no better spot in South Seattle than Deep Sea Sugar and Salt. *11am-6pm Thu-Sun*

Drinking

Classic Coffee Shops

Victrola Coffee Roasters

 27 B2

This popular cafe serves delicious coffee crafted from its house-made espresso blends, roasted at its Capitol Hill roastery (p106). *6:30am-6pm Mon-Fri, 7am-6pm Sat, 8am-6pm Sun*

Cafe Avole

28 F7

In Rainier Valley's Ethiopian enclave, Cafe Avole showcases Ethiopian coffee at its best. *6am-6pm Mon-Fri, 8am-6pm Sat, 8am-4pm Sun*

Alcoholic Drinks, Straight from the Source

House of Smith Wines Jet City

 29 A8

Head to industrial Georgetown to sample

Washington State wines right at House of Smith Wines' bottling plant (which, fun fact, was a former Dr Pepper bottling plant). *2-8pm Fri, noon-8pm Sat, noon-6pm Sun*

Perihelion Brewery

 30 B1

Award-winning locally brewed beers – and accompanying burgers and gastropub-esque sides – await at Perihelion Brewery. *4-10pm Tue-Fri, noon-10pm Sat & Sun*

Delicious Drinks & Alluring Atmosphere

Jules Maes Saloon

31 A7

Seattle's oldest pub, Jules Maes Saloon has been serving since 1888. Once a speakeasy and allegedly haunted, it's a well-worn, comfortable saloon with a contemporary list of local microbrews. *11am-2am Mon-Fri, 9am-2am Sat & Sun*

1988 Cocktail Lounge

32 A7

Located inside the delicious Asian American restaurant Kuma, this new cocktail lounge has innovative, Asian-inspired drinks with ingredients like sesame washed gin and pho-spiced simple syrup. *4-11pm Wed & Thu, to midnight Fri & Sat*

Shopping

Artsy Gems

Georgetown Records

 33 A7

This amazing record store had the guts to open in 2004 when vinyl sales were close to an all-time low. It's an excellent place to score rare picture-cover 45s from obscure British 1970s punk bands. *11:30am-8pm Mon-Sat, to 5pm Sun*

Georgetown Trailer Park Mall

34 A7

These airstream trailers are filled with incredible artwork from local artists. Snag yourself a new painting, a hand-made mug or an expertly crafted piece of jewelry. *hours vary*

Day Moon Press

35 C2

This cozy family-owned letterpress print shop has a small retail area with greeting cards, notebooks and art prints. The rest of the space holds old-school printmaking gear, and the owners will gladly tell you all about it. *noon-5pm Mon-Sat*

See p140
for eating,
drinking and
shopping
listings

Explore
West Seattle

Geographically set apart from the heart of Seattle on its own little peninsula, West Seattle is like Seattle proper's quiet neighbor. You won't find towering skyscrapers and internationally known landmarks in this part of town, but you will find countless cozy boutiques and coffee shops, friendly faces at the weekly farmers market, and a whole lot of charm. Plus, let's not forget to mention Alki Beach, a 2.5-mile stretch of sand along the beautiful Elliott Bay and one of Seattle's most beloved shorelines. This endearing neighborhood exudes a laid-back, small-town atmosphere within a big city, which is its own unique type of appeal.

Getting Around

 Water Taxi

West Seattle is geographically set apart from the other Seattle neighborhoods on its own peninsula, so the water taxi from Downtown Seattle tends to make the most sense for visitors.

 Shuttles & Buses

When you arrive at the West Seattle water-taxi port, there are a couple of free shuttles – routes 773 and 775 – that take riders to the most popular neighborhood spots. To go further, there's a well-connected public bus system.

 Car

It's possible to drive to West Seattle from other Seattle neighborhoods, primarily via the West Seattle Bridge. Parking is often available.

Alki Beach (p138)
GEORGECOLEPHOTO/SHUTTERSTOCK

THE BEST

BEACH DAY SPOT
Alki Beach (p138)

LOCAL MARKET
West Seattle Farmers
Market (p138)

INNOVATIVE FISH & CHIPS
Marination Ma Kai (p140)

FRESHLY ROASTED ESPRESSO
Olympia Coffee (p141)

ECLECTIC RECORD STORE
Easy Street Records &
Cafe (p137)

WEST SEATTLE

Elliott
Bay

Puget
Sound

Hiawatha
Park

ALKI

Bar-S
Playground

Charles
Richey Sr
Viewpoint

For more see

Experiences p138
Eating p140
Drinking p141
Shopping p141

0 ____ 500 m
0 ____ 0.25 miles

WEST SEATTLE

HIGH POINT

SW Andover St
SW Dakota St
SW Genesee St
Fauntleroy Way SW
34th Ave SW
35th Ave SW
36th Ave SW
SW Hudson St
35th Ave SW
36th Ave SW
37th Ave SW
38th Ave SW

SW Charlestown St
SW Bradford St
39th Ave SW
40th Ave SW
41st Ave SW
California Ave SW
SW Alaska St
40th Ave SW
41st Ave SW
Fauntleroy Way SW
SW Edmunds St
SW Brandon St
SW Findlay St

SW Dawson St
40th Ave SW
41st Ave SW
42nd Ave SW
California Ave SW
44th Ave SW
45th Ave SW
46th Ave SW
47th Ave SW
SW Dawson St
48th Ave SW
49th Ave SW

WEST SEATTLE

SW Andover St
SW Charlestown St
SW Dakota St
SW Genesee St
Glenn Way SW
SW Oregon St
SW Alaska St
SW Edmunds St
SW Hudson St

See Enlargement

49th Ave SW
50th Ave SW
51st Ave SW
52nd Ave SW
53rd Ave SW
54th Ave SW
55th Ave SW
56th Ave SW
SW Charlestown St

SW Jacobsen Rd
Beach Dr SW

Me-Kwa-
Mooks
Park

Beach Dr SW

Boyd Pl SW
Chilberg Ave SW
Beach Dr SW

Puget
Sound

WEST
SEATTLE

West Seattle
Farmers Market

SW Oregon St
California Ave SW
SW Oregon St
44th Ave SW
SW Alaska St
42nd Ave SW
California Ave SW
44th Ave SW
SW Alaska St

0   100 m

135

🚶 **WALKING TOUR**

Shop West Seattle's California Avenue

Though Alki Beach tends to draw the crowds over to West Seattle, it's really California Ave – particularly at its intersection with Alaska St – that's the heart of the action in this relatively quiet neighborhood. You'll find coffee shops and internationally inspired eateries nestled next to locally owned record stores and bookstores, all within just a few blocks.

START	END	LENGTH
And Arlen	Easy Street Records & Cafe	0.3 miles; 30min

1 Locally Crafted Jewelry

Start your walk at **And Arlen** (*andarlen.com*), an adorable jewelry store and curated boutique. Its handmade bracelets, rings, necklaces and earrings are minimalistic, while still having distinct elements, like floral patterns and colorful stones. It also works to be size-inclusive and can make your desired size on request, if it doesn't have what you need in stock.

2 Holistic Skincare

Heading south on California Ave, you'll hit **Spruce Apothecary** (*spruceapothecary.co*) before you know it. This holistic, green beauty shop is stocked with good-for-you (and often good-for-the-planet) skincare products. There's also a tucked-away spa section, where you can get a holistic facial and leave feeling like your best, most refreshed self.

3 Your Next Great Read

A couple of blocks further along lies **Paper Boat Booksellers** (*paperboatbooksellers.com*). This endlessly charming locally owned bookstore is somehow filled with all of the best books for every type of reader – an impressive feat considering the relatively small square footage. Author talks and book clubs are regular occurrences.

4 Curated Gifts & Home Finds

Right next door, the family-owned **FLEURT Collective** (*fleurtcollective.com*) is a fantastic place to stop for a gift – or a practical souvenir. From candles to blouses to potted plants, this store is a little slice of homey happiness.

5 Outdoor-Inspired Menswear

While women can get a few new clothing pieces at FLEURT Collective, men will want to cross the street to **Mystery Made** (*mysterymade.com*). Part creative agency, part boutique, the vibes are rad all-around – from the rustic wood register to the 1960s-era motorcycle in the middle of the shop. Stock up on versatile, outdoor-inspired men's clothing and accessories, perfect for exploring the PNW.

6 A Used-Book Classic

Even with Paper Boat Booksellers across the street, **Pegasus Book Exchange** (*pegasusbookshop. com*) has found its own lane in the used-book world. With a particular focus on fiction and children's reads, it's a great place to find your next bookish escape.

7 A Record Store for All

Three doors down, you'll find **Easy Street Records & Cafe** (*easystreetonline.com*). Arguably Seattle's most multifarious record store, young adults with elaborate tattoos mingle with graying ex-punks under a montage of retro parking signs and Nirvana posters. Even Pearl Jam once played at this West Seattle hot spot.

EXPERIENCES

Enjoy the Water Taxi Ride Over BOAT RIDE

MAP: **1** P134 **F1**

One of the best parts of visiting West Seattle is the 15-minute ride with **West Seattle Water Taxi** (*kingcounty.gov/en/dept/metro/travel-options/water-taxi; adult/child $5.75/free*) from Downtown Seattle. In both directions, you'll get stunning views of Puget Sound and the Seattle skyline – from Pioneer Square's Smith Tower to the Space Needle and beyond. Unlike the ferries, you do need a ticket both ways.

Soak Up the Sun on Alki Beach BEACH

Despite its rainy reputation, summer in Seattle is often filled with sunny skies, perfect for a day at **Alki Beach Park** (MAP: **2** P134 **C2**; *seattle.gov/parks/allparks/alki-beach-park*). Lay out a beach towel and soak up the waterfront views, or stop by **Alki Kayak Tours** (MAP: **3** P134 **F1**; *kayakalki.com, from $26/hr*) near the water-taxi pier to rent kayaks and paddleboards for a more active day out on the Sound.

Don't miss **Alki Point Lighthouse** (MAP: **4** P134 **A4**) at the westernmost end of the beach! On Sunday afternoons between Memorial Day and Labor Day, you can even take a tour of the lighthouse, learning about the structure's history and climbing all the way to the top.

Walk or Bike Along the Waterfront Alki Trail WALKING PATH

MAP: **5** P134 **C3**

Pair your beach day with a lovely stroll or bike ride along the accessible waterfront Alki Trail. (Need to rent bikes? Alki Kayak Tours has those as well, for $15 per hour.) Running 3.5 miles (one way) from the ferry dock, around Duwamish Head and to Alki Beach Park, it's scenic all the way through.

While the Puget Sound views on one side will likely keep your attention, don't forget to look the other way at the many charming shops and restaurants. Pop into whatever businesses catch your eye – perhaps the laid-back Alki Surf Shop, the Hawaii-inspired Marination Ma Kai eatery (p140), or the seafood-focused Harry's Beach House (p140).

Pop by the West Seattle Farmers Market FARMERS MARKET

MAP: **6** P4 **A7**

One of the few year-round farmers markets in Seattle, the **West Seattle Farmers Market** (*seattlefarmersmarkets.org/wsfm*) is a great place to experience the city's vibrant food scene and support local farmers and vendors. Taking place every Sunday from 10am to 2pm, you can find everything from organic fruits and vegetables to handcrafted cheeses and baked goods.

There are also a number of food trucks and stands serving hot

⏰ **CLOSED ON MONDAYS**

West Seattle has a slower, calmer pace of life than bustling Downtown Seattle, and that's part of its charm. But that also means that many of the locally owned shops, cafes and restaurants in West Seattle have slightly more limited opening hours. Mondays in particular are a popular day for businesses to close up shop, so either be prepared to find alternatives or opt to plan your West Seattle visit for another day of the week.

meals, snacks and drinks. Sometimes the restaurants and businesses lining the street – including crowd-favorite Lady Jaye (p140) – will jump in on the fun, too. As an added bonus, the West Seattle Farmers Market also usually has parking – a near-impossible find at other Seattle farmers markets.

Hang Among the Old Trees of Schmitz Preserve Park

PARK

MAP: **7** P134 **C4**

The Pacific Northwest in general is filled with greenery, though you might be surprised to learn that many of the trees lining the roads and dotting suburban neighborhoods are actually relatively young. **Schmitz Preserve Park** (*seattle.gov/parks/allparks/schmitz-preserve-park*) isn't that – it's 32 acres of centuries-old trees, perfect for a quiet walk in nature.

While any of the paths are sure to fulfill that need for a peaceful, forested escape, the Schmitz Park to Alki Trail will lead you right back to the action of Alki Beach.

Do note that there isn't any signage on the trails, so you'll want to download a map of your route prior to heading out.

Find the Troll at Lincoln Park

PUBLIC ART

Thomas Dambo is a Danish artist known for his large-scale wooden 'troll' sculptures, all of which are made entirely out of recycled materials.

He has five trolls scattered around the Greater Seattle area, including one in West Seattle's **Lincoln Park** (MAP: **8** P134 **E8**; *seattle.gov/parks/allparks/lincoln-park*). Officially named **Bruun Idun** (MAP: **9** P134 **D8**), this nearly 20ft-tall sculpture is surprisingly hard to locate, especially in the summer when it's tucked under the lush tree tops. To find it, start at the Coleman Pool and walk northeast on the designated trails for just a couple of minutes.

After you've found this beautiful art piece, stick around in Lincoln Park just a little longer to take in the views of Puget Sound, the Olympic Mountains and the ferries sailing by.

Best Places for...

See p134 for map of locations

$ Budget **$$ Midrange** **$$$ Top End**

Eating

Laid-Back Seafood Eateries

Marination Ma Kai $
10 **F1**

Enjoy a taste of Hawaii with kalua pig, kimchi fried rice and *malasadas* (Portuguese-style donuts). The panko-crusted fish and chips is incredible. *11am-8pm Mon-Thu, 11am-9pm Fri, 9am-9pm Sat, 9am-8pm Sun*

Sunfish $
11 **B3**

For a more classic take on fish and chips – though more of the crispy Scandinavian kind than the flaky British kind – Sunfish on Alki Beach has long been a favorite. *11am-8pm Wed-Sat, to 7:25pm Sun*

Harry's Beach House $$
12 **B3**

Laid-back seafood eats await for brunch, lunch and dinner. Try the fresh oysters, both raw and fried. *11am-8:30pm Mon-Thu, 11am-9pm Fri, 9am-9pm Sat, 9am-8pm Sun*

High-End Restaurants

Driftwood $$$
13 **B3**

Elegant beachfront seafood restaurant using local fish, meat and produce. Its interesting cocktail menu highlights local produce. *5-9pm Thu-Mon*

Mashiko $$$
14 **A8**

This sustainable sushi spot has Michelin star–worthy *omakase* (chef tasting menu). Grab a seat at the bar in front of the open kitchen. *hours vary*

Noodle & Pasta Hot Spots

Dumplings of Fury $
15 **A6**

In the heart of the action on California St. You'd be hard-pressed to find better bao buns and dumplings in West Seattle. Don't miss the spicy shrimp and pork wontons. *11am-9pm Tue-Sun*

Raccolto $$$
16 **E6**

Handmade pastas are the star at this local Italian restaurant. Order à la carte, or splurge on the impeccable four-course tasting menu. *5-10pm*

Stacked Sandwich Shops

Gion Banh Mi & Tea $
17 **E4**

Gion Bahn Mi & Tea is the place to satisfy both your boba and banh mi cravings in West Seattle. The lemongrass tofu banh mi is a great vegetarian option. *10am-4:30pm Mon-Sat, 10:30am-5pm Sun*

Lady Jaye $$
18 **A7**

Nearly everything that comes out of this West Seattle restaurant takes a turn in the magic-making, 2500lb smoker known as Cletus. Sit on the patio with a smoked wagyu burger and a smoked old fashioned. *4-9pm Wed & Thu, 4pm-midnight Fri & Sat, 2-8pm Sun*

Little Jaye

 F8

An offshoot of Lady Jaye, Little Jaye is like the breakfast-and-brunch-focused sibling, with its crowd-favorite smashwish (breakfast sandwich with a smashed house sausage patty) and smooth-as-sin espresso martinis. *7am-3pm Mon-Fri, 8am-3pm Sat & Sun*

Sweet Treats

A la Mode Pies

 B7

Enjoy every type of pie under the sun at this local bakery, from classic apple to locally inspired marionberry-and-hazelnut to the blue Hawaiian. *10am-9pm Sun-Thu, to 10pm Fri & Sat*

Shug's Soda Fountain and Ice Cream

 E5

Take a seat in this small, old-school ice-cream parlor for topping-laden sundaes, innovative ice-cream cocktails (a prosecco float, anyone?) or just a good ol' scoop. *1-9pm Sun, Mon & Thu, to 10pm Fri & Sat*

Drinking

Local Libations

Elliott Bay Brewing

 B8

This family-owned brew-pub has a variety of beers – try five at a time with the beer flight. Pair your drink with its take on West Seattle's unofficial dish: fish and chips. *11am-10pm Tue-Sat, to 9pm Sun & Mon*

Revelry Room

 A7

Step into this retro-styled bar for a night of dynamic DJ music and innovative cocktails, like the beloved ube-centered Purple Drank. *5pm-midnight Tue-Thu, 5pm-2am Fri & Sat, 11am-midnight Sun*

Comfy Coffee Shops

Olympia Coffee

 E5

Don't let the lack of square footage fool you – Olympia Coffee has arguably the best espresso in West Seattle. *6am-6pm Mon-Fri, 7am-6pm Sat & Sun*

Sound & Fog

 E7

Puts a lot of care into sourcing great beans, and you can taste it in every cup. Plus, there's a well-curated selection of grab-and-go wines and beers. *7am-5pm Tue-Thu, to 5:30pm Fri-Mon*

C&P Coffee Co

 E8

Has old-school PNW vibes to go alongside its quality coffee and pastries. *6am-6pm Mon-Thu, 6am-8pm Fri, 7am-8pm Sat, 7am-6pm Sun*

Shopping

Friendly Customer Service

Origins Cannabis

 F7

Most dispensaries in Seattle have great customer service, but at this low-key West Seattle weed shop everyone is just an extra bit more friendly and attentive. *8am-10:30pm Mon-Thu, 8am-11:30pm Fri & Sat, 9am-9pm Sun*

WORK SHOP

see E5

With shelves stocked with curated (mostly) vintage items, this home-decor shop is perfect for those on the hunt for antique gems – from old-school cameras to ceramic teapots to vintage tiki glasses. *hours vary*

See p150
for eating,
drinking and
shopping
listings

Explore
Eastside

Across Lake Washington from Seattle proper lies the city's Eastside. It's composed of several different cities, with Bellevue, Kirkland and Redmond at its core. While a couple of generations back this side of the lake was a rather quiet escape from the city, it's now a separate city itself. Big-name companies like Microsoft and Costco have a significant presence here, and many lesser-known tech companies have opted to make the Eastside their home. In response, the Eastside has flourished, with urban green spaces and waterfront sports, adorable coffee shops and tasty South Asian restaurants.

Getting Around

 **Light Rail**
Opened in 2024, the 2 Line of the light rail connects Redmond, Kirkland and Bellevue through a series of eight stops.

 Bus
If you need to travel farther than the light rail allows, the Eastside has an extensive public bus system that can get you nearly anywhere you need to go.

 Car
A car is not a bad option on the Eastside. Parking is often readily available, sometimes for a small fee.

THE BEST

LOCALLY MADE WARES
Made in Washington (p147)

URBAN GREEN SPACE
Bellevue Downtown Park (p147)

OUTDOOR CONCERT VENUE
Chateau St Michelle Winery (p149)

SOUP DUMPLING SPOT
Din Tai Fung (p150)

GREEN TEA TREATS
Nana's Green Tea (p147)

Bellevue Downtown Park (p147)
NADIA YONG/SHUTTERSTOCK

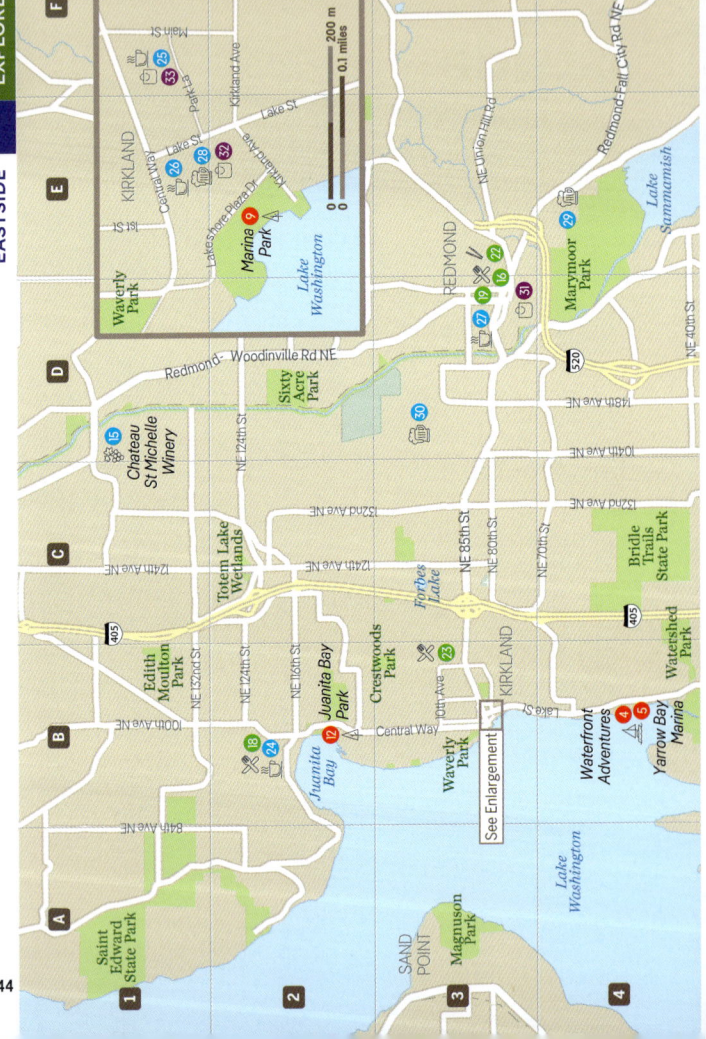

5
6
7
8

Pine Lake

Lake Sammamish State Park

⑪ ▲

F

⑩ Idylwood Park

E Lake Sammamish Pkwy NE

Lake Sammamish

⑥

E

NE 74th St

W Lake Sammamish Pkwy NE

W Lake Sammamish Pkwy SE

SE 34th Way

Weowna Beach County Park

164th Ave NE

156th Ave NE

148th Ave NE

140th Ave NE

Lake Hills Green Belt Park

Phantom Lake

148th Ave SE

SE Newport Way

D

520

NE 24th St

NE 20th St

Larson Lake

Kelsey Creek Park

Blueberry Farm

⑭

Sunset Hills Memorial Park Cemetery

90

SE Newport Way

Coal Creek Pkwy SE

C

Bel Red Rd

Bellevue Botanical Garden

①

Bellfields Nature Park

Mercer Slough Blueberry Farm

⑬

405

NE 24th St

Bellevue Way NE

⑳

⑰

②①

Chism Park

B

BELLEVUE

Clyde Beach Park ⑧ ▲

Meydenbauer Bay Park

⑦ ③ ▲

East Channel

Mercer Island

Luther Burbank Park

A

Fairweather Park

520

② Lake Washington

Bellevue Lake Cruises

4 km

2 miles

For more see
- ⊗ Experiences ▶ p148
- ⊗ Eating ▶ p150
- ⑬ Drinking ▶ p151
- ⑭ Shopping ▶ p151

5
6
7
8

WALKING TOUR

The Quick Hits of Bellevue

When Bellevue was first establishing its roots in the late 1800s and early 1900s, the aptly named Main St became the hub of activity – and things aren't all that different today. Old Bellevue's Main St is still lined with incredibly popular restaurants and shops, and the excitement has expanded outward a few blocks, now encompassing grassy parks and big-brand-packed shopping centers.

START	END	LENGTH
Bellden Cafe	Made in Washington	1 mile; 1hr

1 Charity-Focused Coffee

When you order a latte at **Bellden Cafe** (*belldencafe.com*), it's more than just a cup of fantastic coffee. The cafe donates 10% of its proceeds to local charities, which in the past have included Vision House, a nonprofit aimed at helping homeless families, and Overlake Medical Center. If that makes you want to splurge a little more, order a few bites from the light menu of avocado toast, breakfast sandwiches and acai bowls.

2 Bellevue-Based Dumplings

Continue on Bellevue's beloved Main Str for about a block until you hit **Dough Zone** (*doughzonedumplinghouse.com*). Started in Bellevue in 2014, this dumpling restaurant – similar to Din Tai Fung – has quickly become a crowd favorite with its array of bao, dumplings, wontons and noodle dishes.

3 Matcha Mania

Follow up your dumplings with a sweet treat from **Nana's Green Tea** (*nanasgreenteaseattle.com*). In addition to its lengthy list of green-tea drinks – both matcha and hojicha – this Bellevue cafe has transformed the popular drink into a variety of desserts, including matcha custard-filled croissants, hojicha mochi parfaits, matcha chocolate cake and matcha cream puffs.

4 A World of Colorful Glass

Step into **glassbaby** (*glassybaby. com*), a locally owned shop where the shelves are lined with a rainbow of hand-blown glass cups in every hue. Peruse the range of pale pastels and vibrant jewel tones, calming neutrals and earthy organic shades. Even better, a portion of the profits from each sale goes to the accom-panying glassbaby foundation, which provides financial assistance for people with life-threatening illnesses.

5 A Walk in the Park

Veering away from Main St, you'll find **Bellevue Downtown Park**. No matter the weather, you'll find people walking the circular loop, quietly reading books and saying hello to the ducks swimming in the eye-catching Infinite Fountain. It's a wonderful place to plop on a blanket or bench and just enjoy nature for a bit.

6 Locally Made Goodies

If you're looking for locally made wares, pop into **Made in Washington** (*madeinwashington. com*). While there are a few locations dotted throughout the greater Seattle area, this location in the Bellevue Sq mall has a particularly great collection and layout. Find everything from glass art to smoked salmon to locally roasted coffee at this gem of a shop.

EXPERIENCES

Stop & Smell the Flowers at Bellevue Botanical Garden   BOTANICAL GARDEN

MAP: ❶ P144 C6

Alongside the Washington Park Arboretum (p116) in Seattle proper, the **Bellevue Botanical Garden** *(bellevuebotanical.org)* may be one of the most stunning gardens in the area. It's completely free, and it's filled with all sorts of gorgeous blooms, including irises and dahlias, fuschia and hydrangeas. Spring and summer are the best season to pop by, but there really is no bad time to visit.

Before you head out of Bellevue Botanical Garden, be sure to stop by the gift shop – the Trillium Store – for all sorts of plant-inspired wares, from botanical jewelry to floral-scented soaps.

Sail Away on Lake Washington   WATER SPORTS

There's sort of a running joke in Seattle where everyone wants to know someone who owns a boat – not a huge surprise when you consider how many stunning bodies of water there are in the area.

Even if you don't know a Seattle local with a boat, you can still get out and enjoy beautiful **Lake Washington** (MAP: ❷ P144 A5). With **Bellevue Lake Cruises** (MAP: ❸ P144 B6; *bellevuelakecruises.com; from $69*), you can have someone else captain the ship as you drink BYO wine ($15 per bottle corkage fee) and take in the stunning lake

views. Alternatively, sail away on your own with the help of **Waterfront Adventures** (MAP: ❹ P144 B4) or **Yarrow Bay Marina** (MAP: ❺ P144 B4) boat rentals.

Spend Time at a Lakefront Park   PARK

If hopping aboard a boat doesn't work out, you can always take in the beauty of the Eastside's two bracketing lakes – Lake Washington and **Lake Sammamish** (MAP: ❻ P144 E6)– from one of the many lakefront parks. At the former, there's **Meydenbauer Bay Park** (MAP: ❼ P144 B6), **Clyde Beach Park** (MAP: ❽ P144 B6) and **Marina Park** (MAP: ❾ P144 E2), while the latter has **Idylwood Park** (MAP: ❿ P144 E5) and **Lake Sammamish State Park** (MAP: ⓫ P144 F8).

Soak up the sun, pack yourself a lovely picnic and, if you're really feeling courageous, brave the chilly waters. (Generally, Lake Sammamish's waters are a few degrees warmer than those of Lake Washington, but they're both quite cold year-round, rarely exceeding 70°F.)

Do a Little Bird-Watching at Juanita Bay Park   PARK

MAP: ⓬ P144 B2

If you weren't looking for them, you might not ever know that **Juanita Bay Park** is a hot spot for birds (and a few deer, turtles, muskrats and beavers). Among the towering trees and emergent

☀ BELLEVUE'S FARM ROOTS

While today's Bellevue is filled with tech companies tucked in glass high-rises, early Bellevue was very different. In 1898, the first Japanese immigrants arrived in Bellevue, which at the time was rich farmland. For nearly half a century, these hard-working families grew some of the best produce around – from strawberries to beer hops. Many even sold their goods at Pike Place Market. Unfortunately, trouble began with the Japanese bombing of Pearl Harbor during WWII. In 1942, the Japanese American farmers of Bellevue were forced into American internment camps. When the survivors finally got out years later, most of their farmland had already been sold off to developers, and life was never really the same for them.

aquatic plants, you can find red-winged blackbirds, great blue herons, belted kingfishers, wood ducks and more. Be sure to have your binoculars and camera ready to get a glimpse of the action!

Get a Taste of Bellevue's Farm Past   FARMS

While the vast majority of Belle-vue's agricultural roots have disappeared over the years, there are still a couple of farms holding out: **Mercer Slough Blueberry Farm** (MAP: 13 P144 **C7**) and **Larson Lake Blueberry Farm** (MAP: 14 P144 **D6**; *bellevueblueberryfarms.com/ locations*).

Pluck blueberries right off the bush when they're in season (July and August, $2.50 per pound), or stock up on goodies from their respective farm stands year-round. Fall brings apples galore, winter means beautiful evergreen-based holiday wreaths, and spring features blooming flower bouquets. Even better, both farms are just a 10-minute drive from the heart of

Bellevue, making it very easy to make a quick visit.

Take in Wine & Music at Chateau St Michelle Winery   WINERY

On the border between Kirkland and neighborhood Woodinville lies **Chateau St Michelle Winery** (MAP: 15 P144 **D1**; *ste-michelle.com*). This lavish estate looks like it was pulled right out of Versailles with its French chateau–style architecture and manicured greens.

Throughout the year, the chateau offers a slate of wine-focused experiences, including tastings of its award-winning wines, make-your-own-blend activities, and wine and chocolate pairings. In the summer, Chateau St Michelle Winery becomes a lively music venue, with big names like James Taylor, Stevie Wonder, the Beach Boys, Kelsea Ballerini and the Goo Goo Dolls taking to the outdoor amphitheater stage in the previous years.

Best Places for...

$ Budget $$ Midrange $$$ Top End

See p144 for map of locations

Eating

South Asian Bites

Kanishka Cuisine of India $$

16 D3

You'll find some of the tastiest Indian food in all of Seattle on the Eastside, including at Kanishka in Redmond. With a lunch buffet and an à la carte dinner, it's the best of both worlds. *11am-10pm*

Desi Tadka Indian Grill $

17 B6

Craving flavorful Indian without the fuss? Desi Tadka Indian Grill in Bellevue offers a refreshingly casual atmosphere and loads of veggie-forward plates. *hours vary*

Italian Eats

Cafe Juanita $$$

18 B2

The unassuming Cafe Juanita has mastered the art of Northern Italian fare, using high-quality Italian and PNW ingredients. Settle in for an artful multi-course tasting experience (also available in pescatarian, vegetarian and vegan iterations). *5-9pm Tue & Wed, to 10pm Fri & Sat*

Spark Pizza $$

19 D3

Among the many pizza spots in greater Seattle, Spark Pizza stands out with its diversity of pie styles. You can get a New York–style pizza, a Detroit-style pizza, or a classic Neapolitan pizza here, and they'll all be great. *3-9pm Tue-Thu, 3-10pm Fri, noon-10pm Sat, noon-9pm Sun*

East Asian Restaurants

Din Tai Fung $$

20 B6

Soup dumplings are the star of the show at this Taiwanese restaurant, though the rest of the noodle, wonton and veggie options aren't too shabby either. *11am-9pm*

Monsoon $$

21 B6

Get your fill of modern Vietnamese dishes at this Bellevue classic – though the delicious pho is only served for weekday lunch and weekend brunch. *11:30am-9:30pm Sun-Thu, 11:30am-10pm Fri, 11am-10pm Sat*

Kobuta and Ookam $$

22 E3

This family-owned Redmond restaurant has made a name for itself with its katsu (Japanese breading and frying technique) variations – from classic *kurobuta* (pork) katsu curry to Spanish iberico ham katsu. *hours vary*

Farm-to-Table Freshness

Deru

23 B3

Locally sourced ingredients are a priority at Deru, where fresh produce, artisanal cheeses and sustainably raised meats are the stars of the show. *8am-9pm*

Drinking

A Morning (or Afternoon) Coffee

Urban Coffee Lounge

 B2

Get your coffee and pastry fix at Urban Coffee Lounge. Flavors like caramel, vanilla and truffle dominate the menu and pair perfectly with its chocolate-chip banana bread. *6:30am-7pm Mon-Fri, 7am-7pm Sat & Sun*

Thruline Coffee

25 **F1**

Homey and a little bit old-school, Thruline Coffee has fantastic coffee blends to go alongside its equally tasty pastries. *7am-9pm*

Zoka Coffee Roasters & Tea Company

26 **E1**

It's bright and cozy vibes all around at Zoka – from the floor-to-ceiling windows to the massive live edge table at the center of the action. *6am-6pm Mon-Fri, 7am-6pm Sat & Sun*

5 Stones Coffee Co

27 **D3**

With locations in Redmond, Kirkland and Bellevue, this Eastside coffee company has made its mark with its thoughtfully crafted signature coffee drinks. Don't miss the maple cold brew, known as the Missile. *7am-5pm*

21+ Venues

Flatstick Pub

 E1

With locations in Redmond and Kirkland (and Seattle proper), Flatstick Pub offers a great night out with its cold beers, board games and mini golf courses. *hours vary*

Postdoc Brewing

29 **E4**

Sip on house-made beers with advanced science-inspired names like drag force and luminiferous aether at this welcoming taproom. *3-10pm Mon & Tue, noon-10pm Wed & Thu, 11am-10pm Fri & Sat, 11am-8pm Sun*

Black Raven Brewing

30 **D3**

Black Raven Brewing isn't afraid to experiment, with flavor notes like hibiscus, blueberry and even cinnamon making an appearance. Even better, its Redmond taproom often hosts the public debut of its most innovative brews. *2-9pm Mon-Wed, 2-10pm Thu, noon-10pm Fri, noon-9pm Sat, noon-8pm Sun*

Shopping

Men's Clothing

ASHER GOODS Co

31 **D3**

Find quality men's clothing – with that signature, outdoorsy PNW feel – at this Redmond storefront. *11am-7pm Tue-Sat*

Seattle Thread Company

32 **E2**

The inventory at Seattle Thread Company is split: half business and half casual. In one section of the store, you'll find impeccably tailored suits; on the other, cozy flannels and lace-up sneakers for everyday wear. *10am-7pm*

Contemporary Art

Parklane Gallery

33 **F1**

Primarily showcasing the works of local PNW artists – and occasionally those of international artists – Parklane Gallery's rotating collection of paintings, sculptures, glass art and more means that there are always new pieces to admire. *11am-6pm Wed-Sun*

★ **WORTH A TRIP**

Tacoma

Thirty miles from Seattle lies Tacoma, a second metro area that sometimes acts as a partner and other times as a rival. There's a certain unpretentious authenticity to Tacoma, perhaps from its industrial roots in logging and shipping or its modern-day scene of burgeoning artists and creatives.

GETTING THERE

Driving and taking Sound Transit's Sounder train are the two most popular ways to travel between Seattle and Tacoma. Once there, you can use your car (though parking may be tricky) or use the city's light rail (the T Line) and buses.

Scan for a full list of transportation options between Seattle and Tacoma.

Wander in Awe at Tacoma's Museum of Glass
Opened a decade before the famed Chihuly Garden and Glass (p78) in Seattle, Tacoma's **Museum of Glass** (pictured; *museumofglass. org; adult/child $22/13*) has established itself as a significant center for contemporary glass art and education. While the former focuses solely on the work of Tacoma-native Dale Chihuly, the latter features the works of several glass artists, in both its permanent and temporary exhibitions. Spend your time wandering through boundary-pushing glass sculptures and watching glassblowers at work in the striking cone-shaped hot shop.

If there's one attraction you absolutely can't miss, it's the **Chihuly Bridge of Glass**. Connecting the Museum of Glass with downtown Tacoma, this bridge features three distinct sections: the Seaform Pavilion, with a colorful collection of sea-inspired glass layered on the ceiling above; the 40ft-tall Crystal Towers; and the Venetian Wall, an assemblage of 109 stunning glass sculptures tucked neatly on glass shelving. Even better, the entire bridge is free and fully accessible to the public.

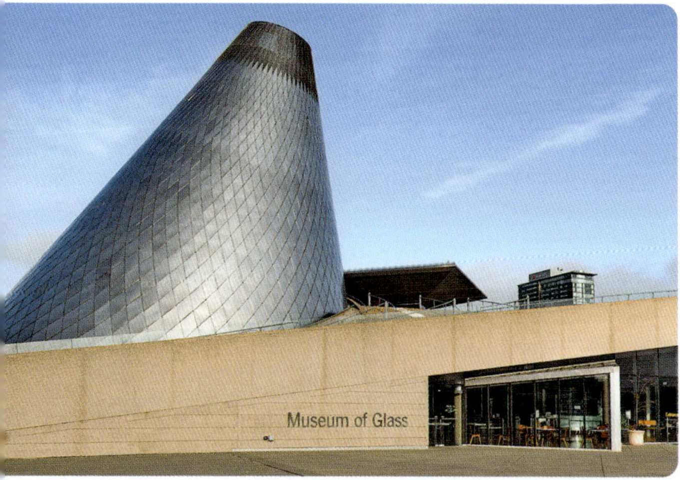
Museum of Glass

IAN DEWAR PHOTOGRAPHY/SHUTTERSTOCK

Get Out in Nature at Point Defiance Park

Point Defiance Park *(parkstacoma.gov/place/point-defiance-park)* may be one of the most gorgeous parks in all of Washington State. Throughout, you'll find old-growth forests of firs, cedars and maples. While it's easy enough to stroll, hike or bike amid the foliage, there are also gems tucked between the trees. Head to **Owen Beach** *(parkstacoma.gov/place/owen-beach)* for some time by the water, kayaking or simply taking in the island-dotted Puget Sound views to your heart's content. Near the southern end of the park, you'll find the renowned **Point Defiance Zoo & Aquarium** *(pdza.org; adult/child from $24/16)*. There, you can befriend a whole host of animals, including red wolves, Sumatran tigers and even polar bears. And in the spring and summer, don't miss the park's beautiful blooms, from roses and dahlias to irises and fuschias.

TAKE A BREAK
While Tacoma has lots of great coffee shops, **Valhalla Coffee Co** *(valhallacoffee.com)* stands out from the crowd with its house-roasted beans and friendly, well-informed baristas.

Mount Rainier National Park

As the most glaciated peak in the contiguous US, Mt Rainier boasts unsurpassed beauty around every twist and turn. Visible for up to 300 miles, the mystical peak has been the grounding soul of Western Washington for millennia. Its original Puyallup name – Tahoma – means 'mother of all waters'.

GETTING THERE
You'll need to drive to Mount Rainier National Park. You'll want to head out early to avoid waiting in line at the entry gates – especially in the summer months, when crowds are at their peak. If you can't come on a weekday, plan on arriving by 9:30am (or after 3pm).

Scan for more information on hours, accessibility, road closures and more.

Seasonal Surprises

At **Mount Rainier National Park** (nps.gov/mora/index.htm; per vehicle from $15), the beauty changes with the seasons. From mid-July through late August, wildflowers like lavender lupines, fiery orange paintbrush and snow-white avalanche lilies rave silently in the surrounding meadows. Late summer into early fall offers huckleberry picking, gorgeous autumnal colors and the calls of elk bugling during their rutting season. In winter, as one of the snowiest places on Earth (669in annually), the roads to Paradise are plowed on all but the most difficult days. Try snowshoeing under the glaciers of the **Nisqually Vista Trail** or on the **Skyline Trail**, or gear up for a cross-country skiing adventure along Paradise Valley Road. In spring, melting snow creates rushing waterfalls and lowland hikes. Don't worry about schlepping equipment. There are well-stocked gear rental locations in Ashford before you hit the park, just west of the busy Nisqually entrance.

Mount Rainier from Paradise

The **Paradise district** (nps.gov/mora/planyourvisit/paradise.htm) may be the most popular part of Mount Rainier National Park. It also happens to be the most easily accessible,

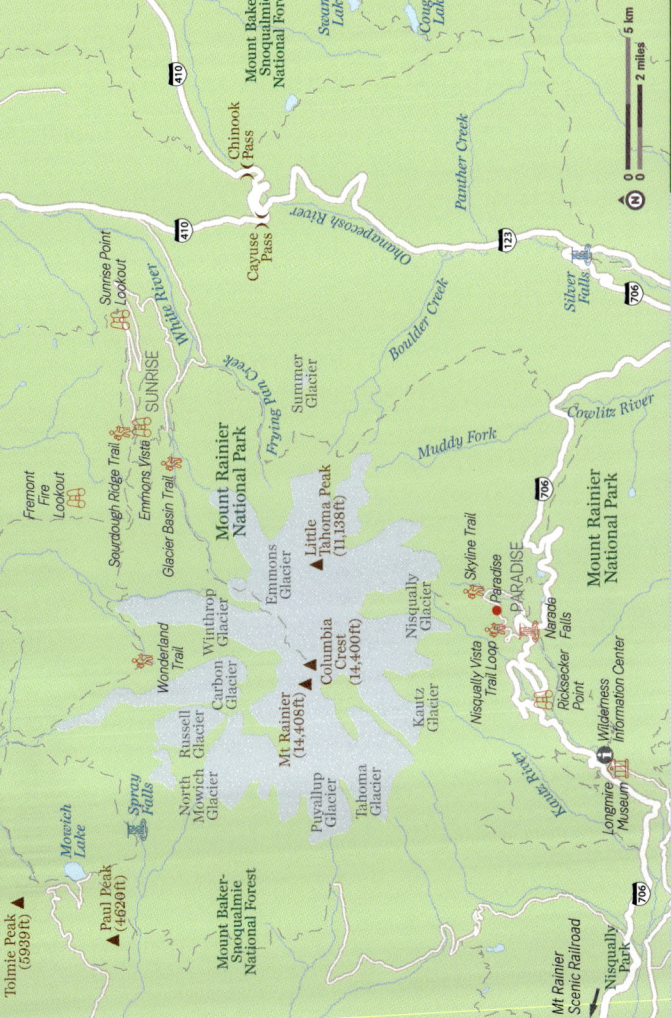

Tolmie Peak
(5939ft) ▲

Paul Peak
(4620ft) ▲

Mowich
Lake

Mount Baker-
Snoqualmie
National Forest

Spray
Falls

North
Mowich
Glacier

Russell
Glacier

Puyallup
Glacier

Tahoma
Glacier

Carbon
Glacier

Wonderland
Trail

Mt Rainier
(14,408ft) ▲

Columbia
Crest
(14,400ft) ▲

Winthrop
Glacier

Emmons
Glacier

Kautz
Glacier

Nisqually
Glacier

Fremont
Fire
Lookout

Sourdough Ridge Trail

Emmons Vista
Glacier Basin Trail

SUNRISE

Little
Tahoma Peak
(11,138ft) ▲

Summer
Glacier

Frying Pan Creek

White River

Sunrise Point
Lookout

410

Cayuse
Pass

Chinook
Pass

410

Mount Baker-
Snoqualmie
National Forest

Seacamp
Lake

Cougar
Lake

Ohanapecosh River

Panther Creek

Boulder Creek

123

Silver
Falls

706

Cowlitz River

Muddy Fork

Skyline Trail

Paradise

PARADISE

706

Narada
Falls

Nisqually Vista
Trail Loop

Ricksecker
Point

Mount Rainier
National Park

Mount Rainier
National Park

Wilderness
Information Center

Longmire
Museum

Kautz River

706

Mt Rainier
Scenic Railroad

Nisqually
Park

N

5 km
2 miles

0
0

155

TAKE A BREAK

Spending multiple days in the park? There are two inns within its bounds, **National Park Inn** *(nps.gov/places/national-park-inn.htm)* and **Paradise Inn** *(mtrainierguestservices.com/accommodations/paradise-inn)*, perfect for an overnight stay.

via the Nisqually entrance. The first stop you'll want to make is at the **Wilderness Information Center & Longmire Museum** *(nps.gov/mora/planyourvisit/longmire.htm)*. Learn about the mountain's history and ask about activities, hiking trails, snowshoeing locations or the **Mt Rainier Scenic Railroad**.

Then, it's time for your official welcome to Paradise. At 5400ft elevation, this small section of the park sees an astonishing 1.3 million visitors a year, here to stop by the visitors center, stay at the cozy Paradise Inn, or park (few spaces after 10am!) and take in the really good levels of beauty. Gape in awe at the 188ft **Narada Falls**, after getting sprinkled with freshwater mist along the steep quarter-mile walk to get there; take in particularly stunning views of Mount Rainier

MELISSAMN/SHUTTERSTOCK

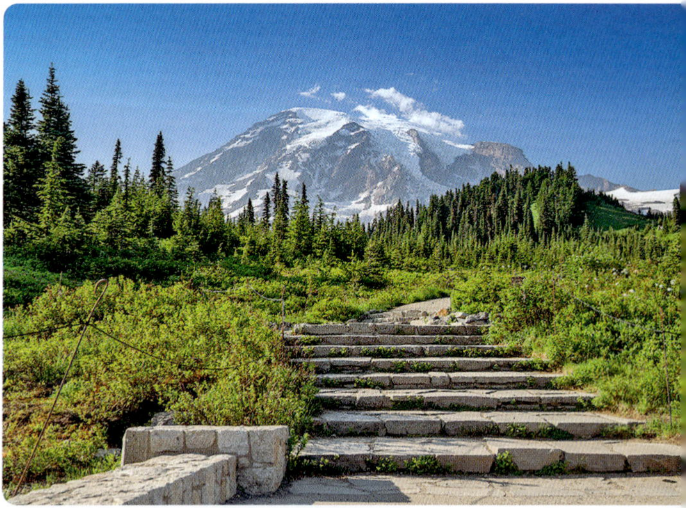

from a little road cutout known as **Ricksecker Point**; or tackle the short-and-sweet 1.2-mile Nisqually Vista Trail, keeping your eyes peeled for wildlife – specifically black-tailed deer and marmots – all along the way.

Mount Rainier from Sunrise

Some 1000ft higher than Paradise, the **Sunrise** area *(nps.gov/mora/planyourvisit/sunrise.htm)* is secretly the favorite of many Washingtonians, and entered via the wending forested drive from the White River entrance (closed to cars for the very long winter). The view from the **Sunrise Point Lookout** is of not only Mount Rainier but the whole Washington Cascade chain, from Mt Baker to Mt Adams. Plus, the wildflowers, glaciers and the Mother of All Waters herself can be taken in with a little more breathing space.

Want to see the largest glacier in the continental US? Take a quick stroll to **Emmons Vista** – or a longer hike along the **Sourdough Ridge Trail** or **Glacier Basin Trail** – to marvel at Emmons Glacier. If you're feeling particularly hardy, try waking up at 3am or 4am for the 5.6-mile hike to the **Fremont Fire Lookout** to take in the sunrise.

Mount Rainier off the Beaten Path

There are plenty of spots off the beaten track, too. Mount Rainier has over 150 trails, including short and easy loops, several wheelchair-accessible trails, and the famed 93-mile cross-mountain **Wonderland Trail**. To hike your own section of the 2650-mile **Pacific Crest Trail**, you can access it via the 3.5-mile-long Naches Peak Loop Trail at Chinook Pass.

MOUNT RAINIER'S NATIVE AMERICAN ROOTS

Prior to Western arrival in 1792, Mount Rainier was called Tahoma, meaning 'Mother of all waters' in the Puyallup language. The mountain held profound cultural and spiritual importance for numerous Indigenous nations, including the Cowlitz, Muckleshoot, Nisqually, Puyallup, Squaxin Island and Yakama. For these communities, Tahoma was a sacred entity intricately woven into their traditions, legends and identity.

Seattle Toolkit

Kayaking, Lake Union (p95)
OKSANA.PERKINS/SHUTTERSTOCK

Family Travel

It's easy to travel to Seattle with kids. There's an abundance of kid-friendly activities – from zoos to museums to boat rides. Even better, your little ones can often get great discounts at big-name attractions.

Stroller-Friendly?

Many Seattle neighborhoods, like Downtown Seattle, the International District and Queen Anne, can be quite hilly. Add to that the fact that other neighborhoods, like North Seattle, don't have the most comprehensive sidewalk coverage, and it can be difficult to get around the city with a stroller at times.

URBAN PARK PLAYGROUNDS

Seattle is big on urban greenspaces, and these parks often have playgrounds for kids. Let your little ones get their energy out running, climbing and sliding to their hearts' content.

A Kid-Friendly Seattle Center Break

You'll inevitably find yourself at Seattle Center for one reason or another – the **Space Needle** (p76), **Chihuly Garden and Glass** (p78), and the **Pacific Science Center** (p82) are just a few of the attractions there, after all. If you find yourself in need of a kid-friendly break, the 'Artists at Play' playground at the center of the action is ideal.

It's About the Journey

With monorail rides (pictured) and water-taxi sailings, kids often find Seattle's public transportation rides just as fun as the attractions themselves.

Kids Ride Free

Kids (in this case, those 18 and under) can travel for free on most forms of public transportation in Seattle.

Admission Fees

Most major Seattle attractions offer discounts for kids, including the **Space Needle**, (p76), **MoPOP** (p80), and the **Woodland Park Zoo** (p118), though sometimes an 'adult' is considered as young as 13 for ticketing purposes.

Accommodations

Given that Seattle welcomed over 50 million visitors in 2024, there are a whole lot of accommodations to house everyone. You'll have your pick of options!

Where to Stay if you Love...

 A Central Location & a Thriving Arts Scene

Belltown (p71) Centered nicely between the attractions of Downtown – like Pike Place Market – and those of Seattle Center – like the Space Needle – artsy Belltown is a popular choice for visitors.

OUR PICK

⭐

We Love to Stay in...

North Seattle (p109) From Ballard to the University District, North Seattle has an ideal amount of excitement. You can easily stay in the quiet nature of Green Lake or take a short bus ride to Ballard and Fremont for trendy restaurants, fantastic microbreweries and well-curated shops galore. Even better, accommodations are usually cheaper in this part of the city.

Being at the Heart of the City

Downtown (p41) A popular option for first-time visitors, Downtown Seattle has a lot of hotel options and easy access to all of the city's public transportation networks.

Space Needle & Puget Sound Views

Lower Queen Anne (p89) There aren't a lot of hotel options in this part of town, but Lower Queen Anne is quiet, family-friendly and within walking distance of the Space Needle.

Dining, Nightlife & LGBTIQ+ Venues

Capitol Hill (p99) This lively Seattle neighborhood is jam-packed with delicious restaurants, trendy shops, lively clubs and innovative craft cocktail bars, many of which are LGBTIQ+-friendly and focused.

Quiet Breaks & Luxury Shopping

Bellevue (p143) Located across Lake Washington from Seattle proper, Bellevue is a bit of an unconventional choice. Despite its many glass skyscrapers, it's quieter than the city proper and is filled with high-end shops.

HOW MUCH FOR A NIGHT IN

Hostel dorm bed
$40-65

No-frills hotel
$130-190

Centrally located hotel
from $250

Food, Drink & Nightlife

⚠ Allergies & Intolerances

Many sit-down restaurants in Seattle ask about allergies once you have been seated. Regardless of if the waitstaff takes this initiative, you'll want to make your allergies clear in advance.

Some Seattle restaurants have made it their mission to cater to those with a specific allergy or intolerance. Dotted throughout the city, you can find a few fully dairy-free and gluten-free eateries.

SEAFOOD SCENE
Being right on the fish-filled waters of Puget Sound, Seattle has an incredible seafood scene. Wild salmon, dungeness crab and oysters are all local must-tries.

SEATTLE TERIYAKI

There's a saying in the city – Japan created teriyaki, but Seattle perfected it. While there are loads of teriyaki spots now, **Toshi's Teriyaki** (p119) was the first to put its spin on the Japanese classic, way back in 1976, adding punchy ginger and garlic to the marinade.

🍄 PNW Flavors

Many local chefs make an effort to use local ingredients wherever possible – a goal often credited to the Native American ways of living off the land. As a result, PNW cuisine evolved, creating a fare heavy in seafood and mushrooms, pome fruits and berries.

Pay the Bill

 HOW TO...

Asking for the bill Most times, the waitstaff will provide the bill unprompted. If not, a quick hand-raise and 'Can I get the check, please?' will do the trick!

Splitting the bill Assuming you don't have an overly large party (10+ guests), most restaurants will be happy to split the bill if asked.

Paying the bill While most eateries have stuck with the tried-and-true paper receipt, many have adopted digital methods of payment, whether that be via remote scanner or QR code.

Tipping When dining at sit-down restaurants, it's common to tip 20%. There is a small anti-tipping movement, so select eateries have already rolled the tip into the menu pricing.

PRICE RANGES

The following price ranges refer to the average cost of a main course.

$ less than $20
$$ $21-36
$$$ more than $36

OPENING HOURS

Bars 4pm to midnight Monday to Thursday, noon to 2am Friday to Sunday

Cafes 7am to 6pm

Clubs 9pm to 2am

Restaurants 11am to 10pm, though hours are highly variable

 Going Out

Coffee culture As the source of Starbucks and home to countless specialty coffee shops, Seattle could be called the coffee capital of America.

Craft breweries Ballard (p112) is a hot spot for craft microbreweries, with more than a dozen establishments brewing up innovative concoctions with bold flavors.

Hidden and exclusive bars There are a few bars around town that aim to stay under the radar, either for the exclusivity of it all or because of a very limited number of seats. Think of the speakeasy-esque Phocific Standard Time (p87) and the 30-seat Deep Dive (p87).

Live-music hot spots Once known as the birthplace of grunge, Seattle's live-music scene, while small, more than makes up for its quantity in quality. Stop by the Gathering Space at KEXP (p85), a radio broadcaster with live performances by fresh indie artists, or the Crocodile (p83), a legendary club that has hosted everyone from Nirvana to Pearl Jam and continues to showcase diverse acts.

HOW MUCH FOR A ...

Cup of coffee
$5

Order of soup dumplings (10 pieces)
$16-20

Fish and chips
$16-20

Half-a-dozen oysters on the half shell
$25

High-end multi-course tasting experience
from $180

Pint of craft beer
$8

Scoop of ice cream
$6

FROM LEFT: PRAISAENG/SHUTTERSTOCK, TYLER TANG/SHUTTERSTOCK

LGBTIQ+ Travelers

Seattle is a progressive, liberally minded city with thriving communities across the spectrum of sexual and gender identities. Approximately 13% of the city's population identifies as part of the LGBTIQ+ community.

LGBTIQ+ Nightlife

While Seattle's nightlife scene is more than welcoming to the LGBTIQ+ community, there are many spaces – most clustered in Capitol Hill – that specifically cater to queer people. Pony (p103) is the most well-known venue, reaching a level of popularity where most denizens either absolutely love or loathe it. Around the corner lies the circus-themed Unicorn (p103), with its jello shots by night and Sunday drag brunch buffet by day. Then there's Wildrose (p103), the oldest lesbian bar in the city. Since 1984 it has been creating a safe space, while also serving up strong drinks and lively DJ mixes. Last but not least, there's Madison Pub (p103), a gay sports bar catering to queers who just want to watch a football game and play a few rounds of darts.

OUR PICKS

Must-Visit LGBTIQ+ Neighborhood

Capitol Hill has long been a haven for members of the LGBTIQ+ community, with its queer roots tying all the way back to the 1950s. Today, the rainbow-crosswalk-filled community is home to dozens of queer-owned shops, clubs, cafes, restaurants and more.

SAVE DURING PRIDE

Many hotels offer discounts for stays during Pride Month (June). While there is a bit of a PR angle involved, it does make it more affordable to celebrate in the city.

SEATTLE PRIDEFEST

Taking place at the end of June, Seattle PrideFest is the city's largest LGBTIQ+ festival, with more than 300,000 attendees each year.

Resources

● **visitseattle.org/things-to-do/lgbtq** The LGBTIQ+ focused page from the official Seattle tourism authority. ● **gaycity.org** One of Seattle's main LGBTIQ+ centers. ● **thegsba.org/travel-out-seattle** An LGBTIQ+ travel resource created by GBSA, Washington State's LGBTIQ+ and allied chamber of commerce.

Health & Safe Travel

As a whole, Seattle is a safe place to travel, but you'll want to be aware of a few things before you go.

EARTHQUAKES

Seattle doesn't have a whole lot of natural disasters. That said, the city is located in a seismically active region and experiences occasional earthquakes, with the last major one taking place in 2001. In the unlikely event of a major earthquake, monitor local news stations for updates and follow the guidance of local authorities.

Vehicle Break-Ins

If you do choose to rent a car during your time in Seattle, it's important to note that car break-ins are quite common. To reduce the risk of an incident, don't leave your valuables inside, whether they are visible or not. Similarly, try to park in well-lit areas and/or in parking garages with some sort of security.

Tap Water

Seattle has some of the best tap water around; fill up your reusable water bottle and go about your day.

Homeless Population

As of 2024, it was estimated that around 16,000 people were unhoused in Seattle. Many of these individuals have made their temporary homes in parts of Pioneer Square, the International District and Downtown. Like in any city, it's good practice to stay aware of your surroundings. That said, please treat those experiencing homelessness with the same kindness you would afford anyone else.

——— SMOKING LAWS ———

Washington State law prohibits smoking in, or within 25ft (7.6m) of, all public buildings. Most state and private smoking policies also prohibit vaping.

QUICK INFO

Alcohol
With the exception of special events, it's illegal to open and consume alcohol in public spaces in Washington State.

Marijuana
Recreational marijuana is legal, but it must be purchased from state-licensed

Headlights On
When driving in the rain, make sure your car's headlights are on.

165

Responsible Travel

Follow these tips to leave a lighter footprint, support local and have a positive impact on communities.

Secondhand Shopping

Vintage and antique stores are all the rage in Seattle – both because these preloved items are sustainable and because they're often one of a kind. Pop into shops like the Seattle Antiques Market (p53; pictured) in Downtown for lovely home decor pieces, Creature Consignment (p107) in Capitol Hill for a whole new outfit, or Third Place Books (p121) in North Seattle for gently used reads.

Public Transportation

The easiest way to travel responsibly in Seattle is to make use of the city's extensive public transportation network. Even better, you'll avoid contributing to Seattle's notorious traffic problem.

Buy Native

Support Seattle's Indigenous communities by patronizing Native-owned businesses, such as Tidelands (p45), Eighth Generation (p53) and Off the Rez (p120). You can buy traditional arts and crafts for your home or sample contemporary Native American cuisine – whichever suits your style. Visit *intentionalist.com* for a more comprehensive directory of Native-owned businesses in the city.

OUR PICK

A Building of the Future

The **Bullitt Center** (p104), a meticulously constructed Capitol Hill commercial office building, generates more energy than it uses. See its innovative systems in action on one of its public tours.

Resources

● **visitseattle.org/going-green** Quick overview of sustainable Seattle attractions from the city's tourism authority. ● **seattle.gov/transportation/getting-around/transit** List of Seattle public transportation options.

Sports & Sustainability

The Climate Pledge Arena (p85) is an incredibly cool venue – and not just because of the talented sports teams that call the arena home.

It officially became zero-carbon-certified in October 2023, fulfilling the Living Future Institute's stringent but impactful criteria – and to get there was no easy feat.

Today, this popular Seattle stadium is powered via 100% renewable energy, implements on-site waste sorting to prioritize zero-waste initiatives, and uses captured rainwater to make the Kraken's ice hockey rink, just to start.

WHAT GIVING BACK CAN DO

Sometimes it can be hard to see the impact of our responsible contributions. At the Bill & Melinda Gates Foundation Discovery Center (p82), a suitably high-tech visitor center for the Bill & Melinda Gates Foundation, the effects of the nonprofit's ongoing humanitarian and research work around the world shine front and center.

Climate Change & Travel

It's impossible to ignore the impact we have when traveling; Lonely Planet urges all travelers to engage with their travel carbon footprint, which will mainly come from air travel. While there often isn't an alternative, travelers can look to minimise the number of flights they take, opt for newer aircrafts and use cleaner ground transportation, such as trains. One proposed solution – purchasing carbon offsets – unfortunately does not cancel out the impact of individual flights. While most destinations will depend on air travel for the foreseeable future, for now, pursuing ground-based travel where possible is the best course of action.

The **UN Carbon Offset Calculator** shows how flying impacts a household's emissions

The **ICAO's carbon emissions calculator** allows visitors to analyse the CO2 generated by point-to-point journeys

Accessible Travel

 Seattle-Tacoma International Airport
Starting at Seattle-Tacoma International Airport (SEA), Seattle works to be inclusive and accessible. This airport has a designated low-sensory room, offers free navigational guidance for vision-impaired travelers via the Aira app, and offers Hidden Disabilities Sunflower Lanyards to those who may need a little extra assistance.

 Bus Accessibility
Around 80% of Metro's buses are equipped with wheelchair lifts. Timetables marked with an 'L' indicate wheelchair accessibility. Be sure to let the driver know if you need your stop to be called and, if possible, pull the cord when you hear the call.

OUR PICK

The **Woodland Park Zoo** (p118) works hard to make everyone feel included. For visually impaired visitors, it offers trained sighted guides, who help with navigation, read the signs, and describe the animals and exhibits. (Please request a sighted guide 14 days in advance.) For neuro-divergent guests, this inclusive zoo has various sensory spaces – including 'quiet corners' and 'romping ranges' – along with complimentary sensory tools such as weighted items, sensory brushes, fidget toys and noise-cancelling headphones.

 WHEELCHAIR-ACCESSIBLE ATTRACTIONS
Many of Seattle's main attractions are wheelchair-accessible, including the Space Needle (p76), the Seattle Great Wheel (p45), the Skyview Observatory at the Columbia Center (p50) and Argosy Cruises' *Salish Explorer* ship.

MoPOP Sensory Days
MoPOP (p80) offers sensory-friendly days and mornings. During these designated hours, the museum is closed to the general public, and the exhibits have lowered volume and light levels.

— **5TH AVENUE THEATER ACCOMMODATIONS** —

5th Avenue Theater (p50) provides ASL interpretation and open captioning for hearing-impaired guests, and audio descriptions via the Sennheiser system for visually impaired guests. These services are only available at select performances.

Resources
● **visitseattle.org/visitor-information/accessible-city** The Visit Seattle tourism office provides a dedicated accessibility page that can serve as a great starting point for planning an accessible visit.

Nuts & Bolts

Opening Hours

Banks 9am to 5pm Monday to Friday, some to 1pm on Saturday

Bars 4pm to midnight Monday to Thursday, noon to 2am Friday to Sunday

Cafes 7am to 6pm

Clubs 9pm to 2am

Parks Generally open 24 hours, though specific facility hours may vary

Pharmacies 9am to 7pm Monday to Friday, noon to 4pm Saturday and Sunday

Restaurants 11am to 10pm, though hours are highly variable

Shops 10am to 8pm Monday to Saturday, 11am to 5pm Sunday

Supermarkets 8am to 9pm

QUICK INFO

Time zone
GMT minus 7 or 8 hours

Country code
+1

Emergency number
911

Population
755,000

ELECTRICITY
120V/60Hz

Public Holidays

New Year's Day
January 1

Martin Luther King Jr Day
Third Monday in January

Presidents' Day
February 17

Memorial Day
Last Monday in May

Juneteenth
June 19

Independence Day
July 4

Labor Day
September 1

Indigenous Peoples' Day
Second Monday in October

Veterans Day
November 11

Thanksgiving
Fourth Thursday in November

Christmas Day
December 25

 ## Toilets

Public toilets abound in Seattle. You'll find them mostly in shopping malls and public parks. They are nearly always free of charge. If you're in a pinch, buy something in one of the city's many coffee shops and use theirs.

Index

Drinking

Shopping

Send Us Your Feedback

We love to hear from travelers – your comments help make our books better. We read every word, and we guarantee that your feedback goes straight to the authors. Visit lonelyplanet.com/contact to submit your updates and suggestions.

Note: We may edit, reproduce and incorporate your comments in Lonely Planet products such as guidebooks, websites and digital products, so let us know if you are happy to have your name acknowledged. For a copy of our privacy policy visit lonelyplanet.com/legal.

Acknowledgements

Front-cover photograph: Space Needle building, Wirestock Creators/ Shutterstock
Back-cover photograph: Pike Place Market, Syrene Photography/ Shutterstock

THIS BOOK

The 4th edition of Lonely Planet's Pocket Seattle guidebook was researched and written by Sarah Etinas. The previous edition was written by Robert Balkovich. This guidebook was produced by the following:

Destination Editor
Melissa Yeager

Coordinating Editor
Andrea Dobbin

Cartographer
Julie Sheridan

Production Editor
Claire Rourke

Image Editor
Clara Monitto

Assisting Editors
Melanie Dankel, Helen Koehne, Vicky Smith

Cover Researcher
Rhia Hylton

Thanks to
Kellie Langdon, Darren O'Connell, Saralinda Turner

Although the authors and Lonely Planet have taken all reasonable care in preparing this book, we make no warranty about the accuracy or completeness of its content and, to the maximum extent permitted, disclaim all liability arising from its use.

Published by Lonely Planet Global Limited
CRN 554153
4th edition – Jan 2026
ISBN 978 1 83758 420 8
© Lonely Planet 2026
10 9 8 7 6 5 4 3 2 1
Printed in Malaysia